BOB ACTON

AROUND NEWQU

Newquay Harbour   (Walk 5)

Circular Walks from Bedruthan to Holywell

First published 1990.   Second edition, revised and enlarged, 1993.

LANDFALL PUBLICATIONS
Landfall, Penpol, Devoran, Truro, Cornwall TR3 6NW
Telephone: Truro (0872) 862581
in association with The Gallery of Old Newquay

A CIP catalogue record for this book is available
from the British Library.

ISBN 1 873443 07 2

MY THANKS TO .....

all those people - too many to name - who generously gave of their time to tell
me about the history of their house, their village or some other feature, or who
helped me find a footpath. Nearly everywhere I went I found people with an
infectious enthusiasm for and detailed knowledge of local history, such as Mr
H. Baker of Nanswhyden Farm, Mr Whale of Porth Post Office, Mr Steve
Kerton of Newquay, Ms Wendy Roper on Pentire Point East, Mr and Mrs
Watts at Trevarrian, Mrs Mogridge at Crantock, Mr Rickard at Bridge (St
Columb Major), Mr and Mrs Schofield at Trerice Mill, the Rev. J. G. Slee at
St Mawgan and Mr Philip Childs of St Agnes, who provided facts about
RAF St Mawgan. Two people above all have helped me, namely Mrs K. M.
Aldis at Crantock, who gave my wife and me a conducted tour of this
fascinating village and wrote two long letters crammed with detailed
information; and Mr Steve Hebdige of Newquay, who checked through the
entire text of the first edition and made many useful corrections and
additions. I first met Mr Hebdige at the Gallery of Old Newquay, where I
can always rely on a friendly welcome and help with all my enquiries from
Mrs Joyce Greenham and others. Mrs Janet Burt and Mr Gerry Walters of
the Newquay Footpaths and Open Spaces Committee, and Mr Roger Lacy of
Newquay, have given me valuable help in preparing this new edition. I am
particularly grateful to Mr Lacy for allowing me to use old photographs from
his collection. The writers whose publications have proved useful are listed at
the back of the book. Finally, of course, thanks to my wife, Viv, for her
companionship on many of the walks (hence my occasional use of "we":
nothing regal is implied!), keen support for the project and help with
historical background.

Typesetting, maps and drawings by Bob Acton
Printed by the Troutbeck Press
and bound by R. Booth Ltd., Antron Hill, Mabe, Penryn, Cornwall

CONTENTS

KEY MAP .... 4 - 5
INTRODUCTION 6
WALK 1: Pentire Farm, Tregona, St Eval Church,
    Bedruthan Steps, Park Head and Porth Mear 7
WALK 2: The Vale of Lanherne:
    St Columb Major to the Sea - and Back 16
WALK 3: Trevarrian, the Coast and Tregurrian 26
WALK 4: St Columb Minor, Watergate and Trevelgue Head 30
WALK 5: Newquay Itself: A Beach and Seafront Walk 38
WALK 6: Newquay, the Gannel, Pentire Point East and Towan Head .. 47
WALK 7: Newquay (Trenance), the Gannel, Crantock and Trevemper . 56
WALK 8: Crantock, Holywell, the Kelseys, Porth Joke
    and West Pentire 61
WALK 9: Trerice, Gwills and Trewerry Mill. 70
WALK 10: Colan Church, Fir Hill, Tregoose and Lady Nance,
    with a possible extension to Porth reservoir and Melancoose 74
FURTHER READING 80
LANDFALL BOOKS ALREADY PUBLISHED ... Inside back cover

IMPORTANT NOTE

I have done my best to ensure that all the routes are on public rights of way, and are practicable and unobstructed. If problems arise, either through errors on my part or because of changes such as the removal of field boundaries, the erection of new fences or the collapse of footbridges, I should be grateful to hear about them. In the final analysis, the decision about where to walk must rest with the reader, and I cannot accept responsibility for problems that may arise through following the routes recommended.

NOTE TO THE SECOND EDITION

In the two-and-a-half years that have passed since *Around Newquay* was first published a good many changes have taken place which affect the walks recommended, as I discovered by "doing" most of them again. I have also picked up a lot more information about the background to the places visited, partly because my library of local books has grown, but also because several readers of the original book have been kind enough to contact me to offer suggestions and corrections. The most constructive of all the suggestions came in the form of additional walk routes, and one of those has materialised in the form of Walk 7. Inevitably there are still plenty of mistakes and unfortunate omissions, and I'm looking forward to further feed-back in preparation for the third edition!

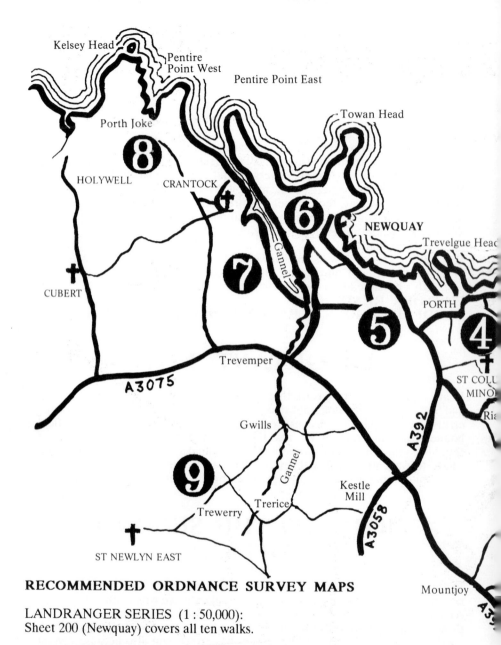

RECOMMENDED ORDNANCE SURVEY MAPS

LANDRANGER SERIES (1 : 50,000):
Sheet 200 (Newquay) covers all ten walks.

PATHFINDER SERIES (1 : 25,000):
Sheet 1346 (Newquay) covers Walks 2, 3, 4, 5 and 10 plus parts of
    Walks 1, 6 and 7.
Sheet 1352 (Perranporth) covers Walk 8 plus the rest of Walks 6 and 7.
A small part of Walk 1 is on the Padstow and Wadebridge sheet, and
    Walk 9 is on the St Newlyn East sheet.

Key Map

Park Head

Porth Mear

PORTHCOTHAN

Pentire Farm

WATERGATE BAY

Bedruthan Steps

1

Tregona

B3276

Trenance

MAWGAN PORTH

3

Trevarrian

St Eval

Tregurrian

ST MAWGAN

N

A3059

2

PORTH RESERVOIR

lan

10

ST COLUMB MAJOR

A39

SKETCH MAP ONLY – NOT TO SCALE

INTRODUCTION

My favourite walks book is J.R.A.Hockin's *Walking in Cornwall,* first published in 1936. "I mean no disrespect," he writes, "to Cornwall's premier watering place, which has grander cliffs and finer beaches and more of both and less valetudinarian stuffiness than any other resort of its standing in England" ..... But the only advice he gives about Newquay to walkers concerns "the problem of avoiding it". I have lived within 25 miles of Newquay for the last 22 years, and until a few months ago I had "avoided it" almost completely, in the belief that the town is overcrowded all summer and ugly all year. Then in June 1989 I paid a visit, hoping to sell copies of my new book, which dealt with an area a little further west. "Yes," said the lady at the Tourist Information Centre, "we'll take some - but what we really want is a book of walks around Newquay." For some years my wife and I had known and loved Bedruthan, St Columb Major, St Mawgan, Trerice and Polly Joke, but now we stayed for a fortnight a few miles south of Newquay, studied the maps and started exploring in earnest. Within a few days we had a whole new collection of favourite places: Colan and Fir Hill, Trewerry, Crantock, the Gannel, Lawrey's Mill, Trevelgue, Park Head and Porth Mear ..... finally we braved the August crowds in Newquay itself and discovered not just the beauty and grandeur of the scenery but fascinating evidence of man's activities, ranging from the primitive burial mounds at Barrowfields, through the ventures of miners, engineers and fishermen in the 18th and 19th centuries, to the development of the holiday resort during the past century. Even in August and in glorious weather we could be almost alone on Towan Head, and easily find a spare seat at Killacourt, in the heart of the town, to rest awhile, eat the excellent pasties we'd bought just a few yards away, and ask ourselves why we'd never done this before. In the course of researching details I returned to places like the harbour, Fistral and the Huer's Hut several times during autumn and winter, and always found new reasons to be glad I'd come back. I hope this book will convey to its readers some of the enjoyment we had in compiling it.

Each walk description starts with a general comment on the special attractions and items of interest on that particular walk, plus practical points about difficulties you might encounter or preparations you should make. Next come brief remarks on how to get to the starting point by car and public transport; and finally the directions for the walk itself, divided into sections which are numbered to correspond with points on the map. An asterisk (*) indicates that there is a boxed note on this point. The maps are merely rough sketches with no claim to close accuracy, and I strongly advise that you take the relevant Ordnance Survey map on the walks. For details, see the note on the Key Map.

Bob Acton

January 1990

6

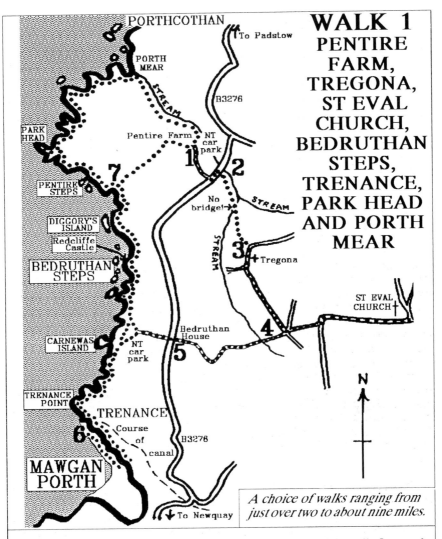

PORTHCOTHAN

To Padstow

PORTH
MEAR

B3276

PARK
HEAD

Pentire Farm
NT car park

7

1 2

PENTIRE
STEPS

No bridge!→

STREAM

DIGGORY'S
ISLAND

Redcliffe
Castle

STREAM

3 ↑Tregona

BEDRUTHAN
STEPS

ST EVAL
CHURCH ✝

CARNEWAS
ISLAND

NT car park

Bedruthan
House

5

4

TRENANCE
POINT

TRENANCE

N

6

Course
of
canal

B3276

MAWGAN
PORTH

↓ To Newquay

WALK 1
PENTIRE FARM, TREGONA, ST EVAL CHURCH, BEDRUTHAN STEPS, TRENANCE, PARK HEAD AND PORTH MEAR

A choice of walks ranging from just over two to about nine miles.

If you've got the time and the energy to do the full nine-mile walk, I strongly recommend it, because the inland parts are attractive and interesting for their own sake as well as making a strong contrast with the magnificent coastal section. The whole route is quite easy walking, mostly fairly flat and on minor roads, tracks and well-used paths, but please note that near the start of the walk a footbridge marked on the maps has gone; except perhaps during unusually dry spells you will be glad of wellingtons when crossing the muddy patches on either side of the stream at that point, and there is also a rickety old gate to climb at the same place. After passing through a tiny hamlet - a delightful spot despite, or even because of, its remote-feeling and exposed site - the route is along a narrow country road with marvellous 360° views. Before turning towards the coast, you could make a short diversion to St Eval Church, famous as landmark, seamark and airmark (if there is such a word). It is a beautiful old building, and strangely impressive in its bleak, lonely setting. Another strongly recommended diversion, also included in the nine-mile total, is to go south along the coast from Bedruthan to Trenance and then on to the beach below, returning by the same route to Bedruthan. This is worthwhile, not only for the magnificent scenery, but also to see a very remarkable, little-known curiosity of early industrial enterprise. Bedruthan Steps is one of those places, like Kynance Cove near the Lizard, whose reputation for beauty and grandeur has spread well beyond Cornwall; as the most celebrated piece of coast between Land's End and Tintagel, it is in danger of being over-visited, but the National Trust has done much to reduce the threat of serious clifftop erosion caused by countless feet ..... and few visitors seem to venture more than a few hundred yards from their cars. I think Park Head and Porth Mear are equally impressive, and all the more enjoyable for being comparatively deserted. Refreshments are usually available at Bedruthan House and the National Trust café nearby. The N. T. Bedruthan car park has toilets, and a little way inland from the walk route at Trenance is a general store.

IMPORTANT NOTE The steps down to the beach from the National Trust car park at Bedruthan are now (1992) closed to the public because of storm damage, and there is no likely prospect of their being restored to a safe condition in the near future.

Directions are given from the National Trust car park at Pentire Farm (grid reference: 852709), about a mile south of Porthcothan. From Newquay, take the coast road north (B3276) via Mawgan Porth; the car park is signed on the left about a mile beyond the National Trust sign to Bedruthan Steps. In summer Western National bus service No. 56 (Newquay-Padstow) stops at the Bedruthan Steps turning, and presumably also at the turning for Pentire Farm. Please check current timetables.

These are directions for a walk of about nine miles (about six if you omit St Eval church and the coast south of Bedruthan). Details of several shorter routes in the same area are given at the relevant points.

1 (*For the short walk round Park Head and including Porth Mear - just over two miles - cross the stile at the car park; after two more stiles turn left, and on reaching the kissing-gate at the cliff edge turn right. Pick up the directions at point 7.*)
For the main route, walk back from the car park to the road - the church tower ahead, by the way, is St Eval - and turn left. Cross to face the on-coming traffic: please be extra-careful here.

2 Soon you pass a farm, Efflins, thought by some antiquarians - Charles Henderson among them - to have been the site of an ancient Chapel of St Katherine and a holy well; as the road starts to descend into a valley, go through or if necessary climb the wooden farm gate on the right. (When we were there a newish post for a public footpath sign had been erected near the gate, but the sign itself was missing. I'll leave you to put your own interpretation on that.) Now the path runs straight ahead, close to the hedge on your right and parallel with the stream below. After a while the stream curves to the right; go down the slope ahead to the point where two streams meet and a farm gate has been placed across the nearer one. This is where you need to cross, because the path continues between the two streams. We found that with some squelching across mud on either side we could use the gate as a substitute for the long-vanished footbridge. Some makeshift stepping-stones have been created on either side of the gate in the form of old tyres; they are certainly better than nothing, but you will need to balance yourself with care as you tread on them. Having crossed the stream, go uphill slightly to the right. Towards the top of the field the path runs beside a Cornish hedge on your left. At the field corner, go through the gate on your left and then cross to another gate by a small group of farm cottages. In 1989 we were pleased to see that the public footpath sign was intact at this end, but by November 1992 it had suffered the same fate as the earlier one.

3 Turn right on the road. The tiny, windswept hamlet you're in now is called Tregona ("farmstead on the downs" - basically the same name as Tregony on the Fal) - one of those remote, ancient-feeling spots that reward the walker who's prepared to wander a mile or two off the coastal footpath. Here again there is some evidence of an ancient chapel - but I'm not, of course, referring to the building which till recently bore the name Tregona Old Chapel. This, we were told, was in use for worship until the early 1980s but now belongs to a writer. Notice how just two of the cob walls have been faced with slate: the south and west, from which the worst of the weather comes. Rusty old farm implements lie scattered around. From the chapel you can look north along the coast to the Trevose lighthouse, and as you continue up the road beyond the village the view in that direction extends to Stepper Point at the mouth of the Camel estuary. In fact, the view in all directions is impressive here. To the left is St Eval church, partly hidden by mounds on the former airfield; in the far distance a little to the left of the tower are Brown Willy and Roughtor on Bodmin Moor, the highest points in Cornwall, and slightly left of them again you may be able to make out the first "wind farm" to have been set up in the county, near Delabole. Ahead the skyline is dominated by the china-clay "mountains" around St Austell. Ignore the right turning soon after the chapel. After over half a mile on this lane-like "road", with grass growing at the centre, you reach a T-junction.

4 Here turn right, and then after a few yards EITHER turn left to visit St Eval church (*), returning to this point by the same route; OR turn right to continue to Bedruthan Steps. At St Eval Leather Crafts, on the right just after you have turned right, many of the items produced are made from a stock of reindeer hide which was recovered quite recently from a ship sunk in Plymouth Sound over two centuries ago; amazingly, much of it is still in excellent condition. Continuing towards Bedruthan, you pass pigsties on the left at first, and soon reach Carnewas Farm (pronounced "C'new's", and probably meaning "rough pasture on the hill"). Carnewas is mentioned by T. O. Darke as the site of an old watermill, with a mill pond just below the farm buildings and a "leat and aqueduct" which carried water to serve another such mill at Bedruthan Farm. Continue ahead past the modern farm

ST EVAL AND ITS CHURCH

Nothing is known of the saint, sometimes called Ewalld or Evalld, to whom the church is dedicated. Parts of the original Norman building, enlarged in the 15th century, remain, but over the centuries it was badly neglected, and the tower had collapsed by 1700. So valuable a guide to shipping had it been that the Bristol Merchants made a large contribution towards the cost of its rebuilding (£400) in 1727; it was whitewashed to make it easier to see, and some of the whitewash is still there. Even then, the church continued to fall apart, and reports spoke of the walls and roof-timbers all leaning towards the east under the influence of the fierce sea-winds. In 1889 it was restored at a cost of £1,071 by J. D. Sedding, who took care to preserve as much as possible of the old church, such as the medieval bench ends and wagon roofs and the Elizabethan pulpit. St Eval Churchtown, as described by T. O. Darke in his excellent *St Eval, History of a Parish* (Lodenek, 1991), consisted of a few cottages clustered around the church, with two pubs among them in the fairly distant past. When St Eval Coastal Command airfield was developed in 1938, the cottages were demolished: Mr Darke includes photographs with captions such as "Grey Cottage and Ellery's Cottage, before the bulldozers," and "Bunt's Cottage before he was pushed out." The church itself, as valuable a navigational aid for pilots as it had always been for seamen, survived and took on the rôle of RAF Station Church; services were taken by both the Rector and the RAF Padre. (Ivan Rabey, in *The Book of St Columb and St Mawgan,* mentions that a decoy aerodrome was laid out on Denzell Downs, and that "Lord Haw-Haw" "frequently.....declared that St Eval aerodrome had been destroyed, when all that the Luftwaffe had succeeded in doing was setting fire to a few acres of scrubland.") RAF St Eval closed in 1958, but many of those who served here still hold the church in their affection and help to preserve it. Mr Darke has a good deal to say about the "wrecking" activities in St Eval parish - some of them as recent as World War I, when German U-boats torpedoed many ships rounding Trevose Head. As much as 90% of the employment available in the area was in agriculture; since Mr Darke himself farmed in the parish for many years, it is not surprising that his account of local farming methods is particularly detailed and interesting.

buildings; notice the ponds in the valley on the right - perhaps an enlargement of the original mill pond. A sign on the main road advertises coarse fishing. When you reach the farm cottage, turn left, and this lane reaches the main road beside Bedruthan House, which opens for coffee, teas, snacks and hot meals all year round, excluding only November and perhaps early December.

5 Cross the road with care and continue ahead to the National Trust car park, café and shop above Bedruthan Steps. The café opens well beyond the normal tourist season, but not all year. If you find the shop open, it's well worth going in to buy the National Trust's leaflet about Bedruthan Steps and Park Head, which presents in a very clear and attractive form the main facts about this area; most of my own boxed notes on this walk are based on it. The path to the cliffs starts between the two National Trust buildings, which were once the offices or Count House of Carnewas Mine (*). To proceed

CARNEWAS MINE

The only surviving records of this mine date from the period 1855 to 1874, but we know that at some earlier time a shaft starting at the bottom of the cliff had been driven nearly a thousand feet inland. Carnewas was an iron mine, but copper, lead, silver, nickel and antimony were also found, and at its busiest time it seems to have been, as Hamilton Jenkin puts it, "a very considerable development". At this time Carnewas Island was still linked to the mainland by an arch, and some lead was mined out there. T. O. Darke suggests that the name "Bedruthan" includes the Cornish word "ruthern", red, and refers to iron ore in the cliffs, but Oliver Padel presumes it is a personal name, as mentioned in my note on Bedruthan.

Carnewas Island, with Bedruthan Steps and Park Head in the middle distance and Trevose Head on the skyline

direct to Bedruthan Steps and thence back to Pentire, follow the main path to the right, picking up the directions again at point 6. For the diversion to Trenance, fork left on the grassy track. Now you follow the acorn-signposted coastal footpath, but all the side-paths to the cliff-edge are worth exploring for the breathtaking views they offer. One of the first goes down to a small quarry overlooking Carnewas Island, undercut by the sea. Soon you pass the National Trust Bedruthan sign; beyond the wall is a large area of gorse to the right of the main path, and it seems likely that any surface remains of the Carnewas Mine workings are hidden among that. The "Pathfinder" map shows "Shaft (dis)" near Trerathick Point, about a quarter of a mile south-west of the car park. There is a fine viewpoint overlooking Trerathick

11

Cove to the violently contorted strata on the sheer cliff-face opposite. Beyond the smaller High Cove, the coast path goes out on to Trenance Point, and there is another good viewpoint just right of the acorn sign there. Now you head inland towards Mawgan Porth beach. Before you reach the first houses at Trenance, look down to the cliff-edge and you will see a cutting running along it; further left, the cutting runs through a garden. This gorse-filled ditch was once Edyvean's Canal (*). If you go across to the cliff-edge to where the canal came to an abrupt halt at a 200-foot drop to the sea, and then start walking left along the narrow path between canal and cliff, you will soon see the top of the shaft mentioned in the note. About three feet down is a ledge, presumably intended to support a cover. The narrow path soon rejoins the main one. If the tide is low enough (within about three hours either side of low water), you might like to find the bottom of the shaft. For that, continue down to the beach. The short length of railway track on the left with a small tipper-wagon was used to help move the large quantities of slate required for the walling nearby. The stream becomes a small waterfall at the bottom. Turn right, under the cliffs. There are two small caves close together, and just beyond them a trickle of rust-red water runs from the cliffs.

EDYVEAN'S CANAL

John Edyvean, a wealthy blind gentleman who lived in St Columb Major, secured an Act of Parliament in 1773 to allow him to build a canal from Mawgan Porth to Porth (on the northern side of Newquay) via St Columb Major, for the transportation of seaweed and sand as fertilisers to the farms. (David Szewczuk, in his "Newquay Town Trail Walkabout", writes of the northern and southern parts of this scheme as two separate "projects"; in fact, it seems unusually difficult to sort out reliable information on this topic from the various brief outlines that have appeared in print.) The lime content of the shell-fragments in the sand was a valuable corrective to the acidity of Cornish soils. A shaft was sunk in the cliffs north of Mawgan Porth so that the loads could be drawn up in buckets, and the canal was cut from there to Whitewater, near the two Trenowth farms towards the end of Walk 2. You can trace the course of it for much of the way on the Pathfinder map by following the contour lines on the north side of the Lanherne valley: since there were no locks, it had to stay at the 200-feet level, so look just south of the 70m. line. Work was also done on the cliffs above Lusty Glaze beach, south of Porth, and near Rialton (see Walks 5 and 4 respectively); and I have mentioned in my directions for Walk 10 the possibility that excavation was carried out in the valley above Fir Hill. This southern half of the canal ran, according to Michael Haigh and David Woolgrove (*Exploring Newquay,* 1974), at 100 feet above sea level for about eight miles. Unfortunately, the entrepreneur's money supply ran out, and so did the water, because of faulty construction of the canal banks. Mr Edyvean is said to have died of a broken heart. *Exploring Newquay* states that the canal, or at least parts of it, continued in use "until the early 19th century", and "the area from Newquay to Mawgan Porth became the best crop growing area in Cornwall when the canal was built"; Polsue in his *Parochial History* (1867), on the other hand, says that the parts of the canal that were completed never brought about the benefits that Edyvean had expected.

Edyvean's canal at Mawgan Porth

If you scramble up the rocks beside this you will find a pool of the same water; peer under the low arch and you will see the foot of the shaft, lined with masonry. Presumably access to it was much easier before silt and rock-falls intervened. This place is a vivid illustration of the skill, determination and courage - foolhardiness, even, considering how unstable these cliffs look - of the early Cornish engineers.

6 Return by the same route to Bedruthan Steps (*). The clifftop walk back to Pentire Farm from the National Trust buildings starts along a well-made stone path. At the top of the steps down to the beach (currently closed to the public, as mentioned in the introductory note), a side-path goes out to the best viewpoint of all, close to Pendarves Island. ("Pendarves" seems to mean "oak-tree headland"; most likely the place is named after a person - it's hard to imagine oak trees ever grew here.) Next follows quite a steep climb, and at the fenced-off section you have a graphic illustration of how the cliff-edge is

---

BEDRUTHAN STEPS

The National Trust leaflet includes a clear and interesting account of the geological processes that created this spectacular place, and also a detailed discussion of the origin of its name. There were steps down the cliff once at Pentire Steps, too, so the claim that Cornish legend told of a giant who used the stacks on the beach as stepping-stones is probably a Victorian invention. Smuggling, or more probably wrecking, is likely to have been the motive for cutting the steps. Hamilton Jenkin came across references to ladders used by the miners to scale the cliffs, and suggested that these could have been the "steps". "Bedruthan" is merely the name of the nearest farm, meaning perhaps "Rudhynn's house". People disagree as to how to say the word, but most locals seem to prefer "B'druth'n", the middle vowel being short, as in "but" rather than "boot".

---

crumbling away. The stone walls in this area are worth studying for their "herringbone" construction, which can look most attractive, especially when clumps of thrift are growing out of them. The third and biggest of the islands forming the so-called stepping-stones of the giant is called Samaritan Island, after a 220-ton brig wrecked on it at midnight on 23 October 1846 (not 1886 as stated by T. O. Darke); her cargo of silk, cotton and calico is said to have graced many a Cornish wardrobe and sitting-room for decades after. For a vividly imaginative account of the wreck of the *Samaritan,* the experiences of the two men (out of the eleven on board) who are supposed to have survived it, and the bonanza of its stranded cargo, read Donald Bray's *Stories of the North Cornish Coast* (Truran, 1983). It is said that bits of the wreckage can still be seen beside Samaritan Island when strong currents have scoured away more sand than usual. On the small headland just south of that island are the remains of Redcliff Castle. The sea has carried away most of the promontory which must during the Iron Age have been the home of quite a large community, if the defences are anything to go by. The builders took more trouble than usual to make strong ramparts: they quarried out much deeper ditches than at Trevelgue (Walk 4) and used the resulting stone for the walls rather than loose earth. Near the far end of the beach is Queen Bess Rock; to see a likeness of Queen Elizabeth I in it now requires a strong imagination, because "her head" dropped off nearly ten years ago. From the north there's now a strong resemblance to Queen Victoria as an elderly lady, in my opinion; what do you think? (Please don't feel obliged to write or ring and tell me!) When you reach the National Trust sign, Park Head, the long island close to the cliffs nearby is Diggory's Island; from a little further along the path you can see that this, too, is pierced by a tunnel.

7 *Just beyond a kissing-gate, you could return direct to the Pentire Farm car park via a second kissing-gate beside a wooden farm gate, where there is a National Trust sign. After a wooden stile you have to cross a stone stile on the right, followed by another stone stile and finally one more wooden one on the edge of the car park.*

For the walk round Park Head you don't need any directions, but it's worth mentioning that, so long as you have a reasonable head for heights, you should keep fairly close to the cliff-edge, because this convoluted coastline provides breathtaking views, but few are visible from the main path. (Not too close to the edge, though: landslips are clearly in progress in many places.) "Pentire Steps" on the maps refers to another cliffside stairway, no longer usable (like Bedruthan Steps) because the bottom part has fallen away. The path out to Park Head (*) itself is one of the most memorable parts of this splendid walk; the greenstone rocks at the end are colourfully decorated with lichens, stonecrops and tiny clumps of thrift; and the view in both directions, but especially south, is glorious. (St Agnes Beacon is prominent, and if

---

PARK HEAD

Oliver Padel *(Cornish Place-Names)* says the headland was probably once called Pentire (= headland), like several others in Cornwall. A farm nearby was called Park Farm, possibly because it once had a deer-park. As with so many other promontories on these walks, Park Head was fortified in ancient times - probably about 2,000 years ago in this case - and two ramparts divided by a ditch remain.

conditions are very clear you should be able to make out the cliffs beyond St Ives.) Somehow we failed to notice the remains of the ancient ramparts across the neck of the headland: our attention was claimed by a small herd of cows, some of which looked in imminent danger of falling over the cliff-edge nearby. As you continue along the coastal footpath, notice the Bronze Age barrows (burial mounds) near the path; the most prominent is near the memorial plaque recording the gift of this area to the National Trust in 1966. The next deep, narrow inlet is made the more forbidding and dramatic by the blackness of the cliffs and the fact that the sea has cut out yet another archway. Beyond this the cliffs gradually diminish in height, and eventually the path runs down to the beautiful, unspoilt Porth Mear ("great cove"); not surprisingly, claims have been made that evidence of old smuggling activities has been found in caves here. T. O. Darke writes that in 1989 a hole suddenly opened up in the path down to the cove, revealing what seems to be a man-made cavern, the existence of which was not till then suspected. He speculates that it could have been a cache for smugglers or wreckers. To return to the car park, walk up the near side of the valley - a lovely place in its own right, and all the more so because of the contrast with the violent coastal scenery. The bracken on one side and the water plants on the other, together with the general setting, strongly recall the valley above Polly Joke (Walk 8), except that at Porth Mear commercial developments seem even more remote. After a series of wooden bridges and a walkway of logs, you reach a kissing-gate; now go quite steeply up half-right and cross the stile on the right of the gate near the farmhouse. Walk to the left side of the garden wall, where another stile brings you to a drive. Turn left on that to find the car park.

The Glebe House, St Columb Major (Walk 2)

WALK 2

THE VALE OF LANHERNE: ST COLUMB MAJOR TO THE SEA - AND BACK

One walk of about ten miles, or two shorter ones:
St Columb and St Mawgan:
6.5 miles
St Mawgan and Mawgan Porth:
3.5 miles (See note at end.)

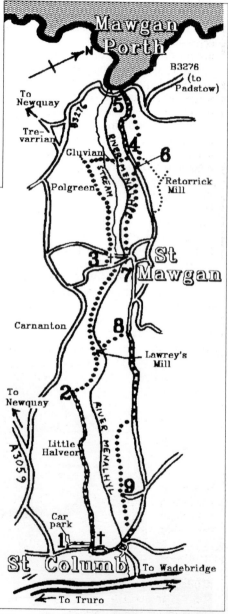

The Vale of Lanherne is famous for its beauty. This walk offers very varied scenery and plenty of historical interest. The small town of St Columb Major and the village of St Mawgan have contrasting atmospheres but both are well worth exploring. Charles Henderson calls St Mawgan "one of the most exquisite places in Cornwall." At Mawgan Porth, nature has provided a magnificent setting for the tawdriness of most of man's contributions to the scene. The walk is not strenuous, although there are some quite steep hills. Muddy patches must be expected, especially near the streams and in farm gateways. Part of the route is on quiet country roads. St Columb has pubs, shops and toilets, and St Mawgan is conveniently placed for a mid-morning, lunch or teatime stop, since it has shops, an inn and a café. Most of the "facilities" at Mawgan Porth are likely to be closed out of season.

To drive to St Columb Major from Newquay, take the A3059; St Columb is signposted after 5 or 6 miles. There is a car park at Trekenning Road, but I suggest you turn left into Fair Street and then take the first left turning (West Street). A small car park is straight ahead. Western National bus No. 92 (92A on Saturdays; no service on Sundays) runs between Newquay and St Columb, but not very often. Check current timetables.

ST COLUMB MAJOR

This old market town was granted a charter permitting the holding of a market and fairs in 1333. Its former prosperity as a local commercial centre is largely gone, and it is too far from the sea to attract many holidaymakers; some of the fine old buildings are sadly dilapidated now, but at least the through traffic which for Betjeman was "unendurable" now uses a bypass, and there are still plenty of pretty streets, such as West Street, with its slate-hung cottages, and attractive corners, especially near the church, where the Liberal and Conservative Clubs are held apart only by the British Legion. Close by stands the Town Hall (1848), shamefully neglected for decades after bits of it had doubled as a cinema, a meat market and a cycle-repair shop, but now restored; it was officially re-opened in May 1992. Barclays and Lloyds Banks now occupy the striking buildings in Fore Street originally erected for the Miners Bank (1873) and the Cornish Bank (1893). There are several old pubs, including coaching inns. On the Red Lion, a plaque commemorates its most famous landlord, James Polkinghorne, Cornwall's champion wrestler. In 1826, at the age of 53, he fought Devon's Abram Cann for the championship of the west. Cann was a year older and at 13 st. 10 lbs was six stone lighter than Polkinghorne, but still the contest seems to have ended with honours even. The sport for which St Columb is best known is hurling, once Cornwall's national game, but now surviving only here. (Hurling does still take place at St Ives, but only in a watered-down form.) Parish records show that it was well established in St Columb by 1594. Twice a year (Shrove Tuesday and the following Saturday week) a ball made of applewood coated with silver is thrown into a crowd consisting of rival "town" and "country" teams, whose aim is to get the ball into their opponents' goal (two stone troughs serve as goals, each about a mile from the town centre) or to carry it over the parish boundary. The contest is hard-fought and even violent at times, and many townspeople board up their windows for the occasion, but the day ends convivially with a massive pub-crawl during which "silver beer" is drunk - beer in which the silver ball has been dipped - unless the winner is teetotal, in which case cocoa is substituted (so Louis T. Stanley reported in his *Journey through Cornwall,* 1958). Perhaps the best-known native of St Columb was Henry Jenner (1848-1934), who did much to revive interest in the Cornish language, and founded the Cornish Gorsedd ("meeting of the bards") in 1928. The slate-hung Glebe House by Church Steps, with its intriguing angles, bears the date 1638. The church itself, dedicated to St Columba, "is one of the finest buildings in Cornwall" (Henderson); it is a beautiful and spacious 14th/15th century building with an unusual tower above open arches. The space below provided useful stabling in the days when many of the congregation arrived on horseback. Inside, notice the old carved bench-ends incorporated in the rebuilt pews. Most of the cost of building the church was borne by the Arundell family of Lanherne. In the south chancel aisle are their tombs and brasses. For a week in late August each year until recently the church was the setting for "Music at St Columb", a series of choral and orchestral concerts of very high standard directed by Richard Cooke, the son of a former Rector, the late Canon Gordon Cooke. Now in August 1992 a welcome attempt has been made to revive the tradition, though on a smaller scale.

1 From the car park you could walk around the right-hand side of the recreation ground, turning right through the wooden gate before you reach the children's playground, then left at the street (West Street). Alternatively, go back to the car park entrance and turn left there. As you approach the church, take the first left turning, Victoria Street. (Or, if you are starting at the church, leave the churchyard by the main entrance, passing Glebe House, turn right up Fore Street, and then first right; this leads to Victoria Street.) This soon becomes a quiet little country road running parallel to the Menalhyl River in its valley to your right. Menalhyl probably means "mill river"; other versions of the name are Malanhyl, Menalthy and Mellanhayle. Ignore all side turnings. After a mile or so you reach Little Halveor farm, and here the road becomes a track through woodland, very muddy in places at certain times of the year. After the stile on the right of a five-bar gate it dwindles to a path. Keep straight on, with the hedge to your left. Cross the stile and the stream where the woodland begins again.

2 Turn right where signposted St Mawgan, and then immediately right again: be careful not to miss the second sign. Where the path forks, keep left, and now you have a pretty walk through the wooded valley down to St Mawgan. Before long you should be able to discern an old leat (artificial water-channel) down on the right, between path and river; as you continue, this becomes more and more obvious, and eventually you may catch a glimpse of what little remains of Lawrey's Mill, whose waterwheel was fed by the leat. Continue straight ahead, following the Public Footpath sign. Approaching St Mawgan (*), turn right at the wooden sign (easily missed) and go through the kissing-gate. Now you pass the tea-garden and shops; the Falcon Inn is on the left, and the Penny Inn is about half a mile up the same road. Just past the Falcon, turn right for Lanherne. Signs direct you to the Chapel.

For the shorter walk, returning direct to St Columb, continue the directions at point 7.

3 To continue to the coast, go through the churchyard. On the left immediately beyond the lych gate is a well, said to be where St Mawgan preached and baptised. The stone trough nearby is supposed to have been used as a goal when hurling was played at St Mawgan, about two hundred years ago: see the note on St Columb. A little further along the path, a grave on the right has an old wheel cross at its head, known as the Pigsty Cross because it was found in a pigsty near Truro. Before the church on the right is the rose garden, and below the east windows is a small ancient cross, Mawgan Cross, which was brought here when St Mawgan airfield was developed. Beyond the church, you pass the lantern cross on your right and on your left a memorial to nine men and a boy frozen to death after a shipwreck on Tregurrian (Watergate) beach in 1846. The Tudor building on your left is Lanherne; notice the decorative heads of the drainpipes, added in the 18th century. Turn left at the road, and almost at once turn right through a gate on to a well-surfaced lane running parallel to the river. The woodland on the right is called the Nuns' Grove. After about half a mile you pass Polgreen Farm, and then the road curves uphill. As you approach the next farm, Tolcarne Merock, turn sharp right on to a bridleway which goes down into

*The Lantern Cross
at St Mawgan*

ST MAWGAN

The full name is St Mawgan in Pydar, to distinguish it from Mawgan in Meneage by the Helford. The great house here is Lanherne, one of the principal seats of the Arundell family for nearly five hundred years. The Arundells were Cornwall's most powerful family in the Tudor period, and at one time or another they owned as many as 70 or 80 manors in Cornwall alone, notably Trerice (see Walk 9). The present building dates from Tudor times, with considerable 18th-century additions. Since 1794 it has been the home of Carmelite nuns, a strict order whose rules prevent much contact with the outside world. According to Charles Lee, "They lead the strictest lives, never touching animal food, never leaving the convent walls, and never seeing a man face to face except when the doctor is called in at the last necessity." The original chapel at Lanherne was probably, Charles Henderson suggests, "of some magnificence", but all trace of it has now gone. The small, simple chapel built for the nuns is open to the public; inside is a silver lamp, presumably a relic of the old chapel, and "said to have been burning continuously since the Reformation" (Henderson). Outside, near the chapel entrance is what Lee claims to be "the finest ancient decorated cross in Cornwall", elaborately carved with twisting patterns on the shaft; on the right side is a long-tailed dragon, its head at the bottom of the shaft. The letters RUHOL on the back are probably the name of the sculptor, who is thought to have lived about 900 AD. The cross was brought here from Gwinear, near Hayle. In the directions I point out the three ancient crosses in the churchyard, the most important of which is a medieval lantern cross with carvings said to represent the Annunciation (west side), God the Father holding the crucified Son (east), and bishops (north and south). The church is mainly of the 13th and 15th centuries. It contains several memorials to the Arundells, an imposing rood screen and a carved pulpit (both late 16th century), and forty medieval carved bench-ends. The *Hodbarrow Miner* memorial board (see the photo on page 22) is at the west end. The Carnanton estate is on the southern side of the village. The medieval manor house and chapel were demolished in the mid-18th century when the present mansion was built. The Willyamses of Carnanton planted most of the trees hereabouts, according to Margaret Trevenna's interesting and attractively presented "Guide and History". She also says that the inn (formerly called the Gardeners' Arms) derives its present name from the fact that the Willyams family crest shows a falcon; according to Ivan Rabey's *Book of St Columb and St Mawgan,* however, the explanation is connected with the fact that the Arundell family were Roman Catholics. After the Reformation, Mass continued to be celebrated privately in the village, and it is said that a falcon was released to announce that a service was about to take place. The Arundells had run considerable risks by remaining faithful to the "old religion": Francis Tregian of Golden near Grampound, for example, suffered heavy punishment for harbouring a Catholic priest in 1577. (See *Around Mevagissey,* page 30.) The Arundells fared better through what Henderson calls "prudent management". They also had the support of the Rector of Mawgan at that time: he is said to have walked to London and back on their behalf "and by that means saved Arundell's estate." Harold Hosking gives a brief but vivid account of his four-year stay as Rector here during the late 1950s in *It's Only the Vicar* (Gooday Publishers, 1987).

the valley, crossing a small stream and then the Menalhyl River by fords, each with a footbridge. The track brings you to Gluvian Farm, sometimes called Gluvian Flamank to distinguish it from Gluvian Marth higher up the valley. A chapel dating back at least to the 14th century was located here; much later, it was partially rebuilt for use as a wagon shed. Its position is marked on the Pathfinder OS map. If any part of it is still standing, it is presumably the more distant of the two buildings up on your left as you approach the farm. Charles Henderson, conducting his researches between 1910 and 1924, found several relics of the original chapel in Gluvian farmyard and "at Windsor Mill in the valley below". (See part 6 of the directions.)

4 Turn left at the road, which leads down to Mawgan Porth (*).

MAWGAN PORTH

This is supposed to have been where the 6th-century Irish Abbot-Bishop Maugan landed in Cornwall on his way from Wales to Brittany; he is said to have crossed the county and set sail again at Mawgan Creek on the Helford River. In 1934 or soon after, an ancient skeleton was discovered during preparations for building work on the area now occupied by a putting green. As a result, the building plans were shelved, but no systematic archaeological excavations were carried out till 1952-4. They revealed the site of a Saxon settlement of about 1000 AD whose houses had rectangular rooms opening on to a yard. The inhabitants seem finally to have given up the struggle against sand blown in from the beach, and for almost a thousand years after their departure the land beside the cove was purely agricultural, with few if any buildings: the farm buildings are either well inland, like Gluvian, or on the ridges above, like Bre-pen to the south and Trenance to the north. (The latter, by the way, is very oddly named, since - as explained in Walk 7 - "Trenance" means "valley farm". Perhaps the explanation is that the bulk of its land was down by the cove.) An article in *The Cornwall Village Book* (Cornwall Federation of Women's Institutes, 1991) tells in some detail the story of how the holiday potential of the splendid beach began to be exploited after World War I, but the photo of Mawgan Porth in the Ward Lock *Newquay and North Cornwall* guide published about 1939 appears to show not one building by the beach. (If the café built beside the bridge in 1932 is there, it must have been very inconspicuous.) After World War II development gathered pace. John Betjeman's *Cornwall - A Shell Guide* of 1964 remarks that Mawgan Porth "is full of new seaside villas and has lost its remoteness". The petrol station and ice-cream-and-candyfloss bars of today have taken it further along that path, but still from the attractive Riviera Inn, up the hill on the southern side, one can imagine the beauty of the place as it must once have been and appreciate the beauty it has retained in spite of everything. One last word for the benefit of mermaid-spotters: in July 1827 the *West Briton* gave a detailed report of the sighting at Mawgan Porth of several mermaids lying face-down on the rocks; above the waist their bodies were coloured "exactly like that of a Christian", but their arms were short and fin-like, and their lower parts were bluish and ended in a tail. Donald Bray, from whose *Stories of the North Cornish Coast* I have culled this information, hints they they may have been seals, but still exhorts serious students of "merrymaids" to "Keep looking!"

Alex Old's dramatic photograph of the wreck of a 114-ton topsail schooner. She was carrying coal from Runcorn to Truro. A board in St Mawgan church reads:
In Memory of Richard Tyrran, Captn, Griffith Owen, Mate, Walter Moulsdale, Seaman and Evan Evans, Boy Cook, who took their last Voyage on the waves of this troublesome world in the "Hodbarrow Miner", wrecked on March 6th 1908 at St Mawgan Porth.

5 The return trip starts along the road you came in by. When you reach the Mawgan Porth Holiday Park, turn left and take the Public Footpath on your right, signposted to St Mawgan. At the junction of paths bear right over the stream, crossing a bridge at a ford, and keeping straight on past the Sun Haven Valley Caravan and Camping Park rather than taking the small road that curves to the left.
(That leads to Retorrick Mill, now rebuilt as a modern house, from which there is a signposted path to the right leading to St Mawgan, so it would be a possible alternative route. It is quite pleasant but involves an uphill stretch on the path and then some road walking. Turn left on reaching the road, then first right - this brings you steeply down to the village.)

6 When you come to the "main" road, cross it and go over the stile opposite. The path goes to the right of a line of bramble-patches to another stile, then through a rather overgrown but very attractive area with overhanging branches, with the river down on your right. A third stile and a kissing-gate beside Winsor or Windsor Mill (two cottages nicely converted into an impressive home in an idyllic setting) bring you to a road leading into St Mawgan, with a good view of the church and convent across the valley. Go down the hill on the right, over the bridge, turn left at the church and left again towards the post office to continue the walk.

7 You could make this a round walk by leaving St Mawgan on the road via Lanvean and Trevenna, but I'd recommend you to begin the return to St Columb by going back up the valley path, starting on the right-hand side of the post office and turning right at the entrance to the car park, then left after the kissing gate. After about a mile there is a left fork towards Lawrey's Mill (*) and a bridge over the river. There was no signpost here when we last walked this route (August 1992), but the bridge is clearly visible from the main path. Unless you prefer to stay on the south side of the valley, retracing your steps back to St Columb, you need to cross this bridge and take the steep path up to Higher Tolcarne. Apart from the stiff climb at the start, the drawbacks to this route are (a) nearly a mile of rather dull road walking, and (b) having to negotiate some awkward stiles and climb a few gates on field paths - and perhaps brave some lively, yapping dogs at Lower Trenowth Farm. Among the compensations are fine views across the valley and town to St Columb church, and a chance to explore the attractive "Bridge" area of St Columb, with its watermills, pretty cottages and historic buildings such as the Old Rectory. The following directions assume you have decided that the compensations outweigh the drawbacks.

8 Turn right on the road at Higher Tolcarne. Continue past Trembleath Farm, and then for about another half mile. Turn right down the drive with signs to Lower Trenowth Farm and Bungalow. In August 1992, these were accompanied by a warning to "Beware of the dogs." If you'd prefer to avoid any encounter with them, you could simply continue along the road, the last mile-or-so of which as it approaches St Columb can be busy. We decided to live dangerously, and were met by the farmer's wife at Lower Trenowth, who

Lawrey's Mill (1990)

LAWREY'S MILL

Charles Lee, in his account of the Vale of Lanherne written about 1903, mentions that the mill-wheel was ruined and the out-buildings were weather-beaten even then. After describing the "idyllic beauty" of the spot, he writes: "old folk remember when a wool-stapler lived here and carried on a local manufacturing of blankets, and the air was tainted with the fumes of sulphur from the bleaching-shed, and one of the fields above (still known as Reek-Park) was white with blankets stretched to dry on their recks or frames." Despite the sad state of the mill buildings in 1989, you could still clearly see where the overshot waterwheel was: the square hole in the wall opposite the lean-to entrance porch of the house carried its axle, and the leat fed it from the bank above. By August 1992 a fence had been erected near the bridge, preventing access to the site, and I am told that most if not all of the mill has now been demolished on the grounds that it had become dangerous.

Lawry's Mill, Mawgan, Cornwall.   Argall's Series

My dear A. How do you like this view, pretty is'nt it. I am so glad you are taking a holiday, for you needed one badly do make the most of it and go out all you can. Love from Annie!

The mill was a favourite subject for Victorian and Edwardian photographers. This card was posted in Truro on October 6th 1903.

called the dogs off and gave us friendly guidance. Go through the farmyard (you may have to climb the gate), and then take the right-hand wooden gate. Now keep the hedge on your left, and go through the gap up to the high hedge, where you will see St Columb church ahead. At the next hedge the stile in the corner may be hidden by vegetation and a low fence. After this, still keep the hedge on your left at first, but at the field-end go through (or, more likely, over) the newish metal gate on the left, and continue with the hedge to your right. After another metal gate (this one actually opens!), you will come to Higher Trenowth or Trenoweth, where there are two five-bar gates in quick succession.

9 Cross the concrete drive, continue ahead and cross the stile to the left of the gap between walls. (Corrugated iron had been placed in front of the stile, but with a little effort the piece blocking the way could be slid aside.) Walk with the hedge on the right. Cross the stile on the right at the corner (steps down) and then walk with the hedge and quite a deep ditch on your left. Go over the footbridge and awkward, rickety stile at the corner, then straight across the middle of the field to a stone bridge and stile at the next hedge; keep straight on to yet another stile, this time with two bridges, apparently made from old railway sleepers; now go right then left in front of a small barn. By now you have a good view of the church, and in the valley between you and the church is the Old Rectory, a moated house probably dating back to the early 14th century but rebuilt in 1851 in the "Gothick" style. This was at the time when plans for creating a Bishop of Cornwall were being discussed; St Columb was short-listed as a possible ecclesiastical centre for the county, and the Old Rectory was enlarged to serve as the Bishop's Palace. In recent years it was a hotel; in August 1992 it re-opened as the St Columb Meadery. A grassy track brings you to a stile beside a metal gate, and the tree-lined lane leads to the road on the northern side of St Columb. Turn right to return to church and car park. Notice the old toll house (a relic of the days when this was the main road from St Columb to Wadebridge) and Town Mills by the bridge, and the leat beside the Menalhyl River there. "Except for its church," loftily stated the old Ward Lock guide in its entry on St Columb Major, "the place has little of interest." Presumably no-one showed the anonymous author this part of it. At least three waterwheels once operated nearby: at Town Mills (later used as a coal-store, as a faded old sign still testifies; in the former coal-yard is an intriguing little building which looks as if it was modelled on Noah's Ark); at the Old Rectory; and at the Tuckingmill, whose name suggests it was used for the cleaning or fulling of wool, although Mr Edgar Rickard, who lives nearby, remembers corn being ground there. This mill, now named Thirlby Mill, is a little way upstream, near the Retreat Hospital. Its present owner, Mr Thirkell, is installing a new wheel, and hopes eventually to restore the mill to full working order; apparently all the internal "works" are still intact. A millpool and various leats can still be seen close by. If you still have the time and energy to manage a short diversion, I recommend you to take the side-road beside the river, starting beside the toll house. Among the pretty cottages here, one - No. 25 - was the birthplace of Jack Crapp, the first Cornishman to play cricket for England; a plaque gives the details. When you reach the main road, cross and continue uphill a little further on the road signed to The Retreat, which soon brings you to Thirlby Mill. Return the same way.

For the round walk from St Mawgan to the coast and back, follow the directions from points 3 to 6. To park at St Mawgan, turn right immediately beyond the Falcon Inn (assuming that you are approaching from Newquay) and go to the right of the post office/store. Caution: the sleeping policemen could be a severe test of your car's suspension!

WALK 3
TREVARRIAN, THE COAST AND TREGURRIAN

About two and a half miles;
a little more if you extend the coastal walk towards Mawgan Porth.

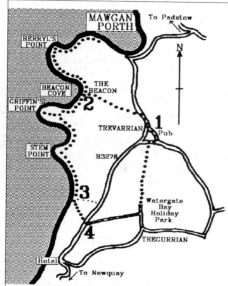

This easy, short walk features splendid cliff scenery and pleasant inland walking with panoramic views both of the coast and across country. The two hamlets on the route are both old farming and fishing communities where modern residential housing and holiday developments blend well, for the most part, with the original stone or cob cottages and farm buildings. Both suffer the consequences of being on busy holiday routes, but my suggested walk manages to avoid the main roads almost completely. I have picked Trevarrian as the start-and-end point mainly because walkers might welcome some fortification before and/or after their excursion at its pleasant pub, the Travellers Rest, which serves a good range of food. Despite being quite large, it manages to retain a cosy atmosphere, perhaps partly because the main part of it was originally two fishermen's cottages. As mentioned below, there is room for a little roadside parking at the start of the route - and then, of course, there's the pub car park for customers. Both Trevarrian and Tregurrian are served by Western National bus services 53 and 56 from Newquay, but these run only in the season; check current timetables. Some parts of the inland tracks and paths were muddy when we were there, but not as bad as might have been expected, considering the deluges there had been during the previous few days. The path from Tregurrian to Trevarrian looked little-used: part had been ploughed up and not yet reinstated, and one stile was partially blocked by garden equipment. The coastal section involves a few steep climbs, and is too exposed to be safe in very high winds.

Trevarrian is near Mawgan Porth on the B3276 from Newquay. Driving from Newquay, if you take the inland road from the Watergate Bay Hotel and go through Tregurrian, you will pass the Travellers Rest, but if you keep to the coast road you would need to turn right in Trevarrian for the pub. The walk starts on the Mawgan Porth side of the village, and there is a small roadside parking space near the point where the seaward track begins.

Tregurrian as it was in the 1920s. (Photograph by A. H. Hawke)

1 From the pub, continue along the main road bearing right towards Mawgan Porth and turn left at the Public Footpath sign on to a grassy track running between hedges towards the coast. At the end of this, turn left where there is (or was) a broken footpath sign, and keep by the hedge on the left to a redundant concrete-block stile. This place is called the Beacon (*), and below you is Beacon Cove.

THE BEACON AND BEACON COVE

If you look south-west from here on a clear day, on the skyline almost exactly above the huge white hotel (The Atlantic) which dominates Newquay you will see St Agnes Beacon. The Atlantic Hotel itself stands beside an area known as The Beacon. In previous centuries the lighting of fires on a chain of tall hills, mostly still called beacons, was used as a system of communication at times of emergency or celebration; probably the best-known occasion involving S. W. England was the sighting of the Spanish Armada near Lizard Point, although it was too misty in Cornwall that night for the system to work well. In 1988 the beacons were again lit to mark "Armada 400"; appropriately, there was thick mist again, plus gales and pouring rain. I was on St Agnes Beacon at the time, and I'm pretty sure no-one could have seen fire-signals from any other hill.... certainly not from the Beacon you're now on, anyway, because for some reason it wasn't included in the celebrations. Beacon Cove, so I was told by a local couple, was once the scene of busy quarrying activity, and supplied much of the stone for the older buildings in St Columb Major. On the cliffs at the cove an iron lode (vein) is exposed, and some mining was carried out.

---

2 From here the main walk route goes left along the coastal footpath, but it's well worth going a little way in the opposite direction first. After a few hundred yards, the lower path leads down to Berryl's Point, where there is a fairly new-looking granite block with an anchor carved on it; I hope that any reader who knows what this is will tell me. (Two years later, no one has!) A little further round, you have a fine view of Mawgan Porth, with sheer cliffs on the near side and a big cave near the headland opposite (Trenance Point). As you approach Beacon Cove again on the way back you have the clearest view of the ancient fortifications on Griffin's Point (*), on the far side of the cove; and inland St Eval church tower stands out clearly. Continue along the coast path round to the far side of the cove. Before crossing the bridge, it's

---

GRIFFIN'S POINT

Cornwall has many cliff-castles dating from roughly 200 BC to 100 AD. Headlands like this were fortified with ramparts and ditches - two of each in this case - to protect small settlements; presumably at Griffin's Point, as at Redcliff Castle (Walk 1), cliff-falls have destroyed much of the area where huts once stood. If you look back at this headland from Stem Cove, to the south, you will see two cavities in the cliff-face; at least one of these is probably a "gunnis" or old mine-working which exploited a lead lode.

The cliff castle at Griffin's Point, as seen from the Beacon. On the skyline beyond Newquay is St Agnes Beacon.

worth going out beside the stream to where it tumbles over the cliff-edge; and again at the top of the steps beyond the bridge it's worth taking the path out to Griffin's Point. Now the coast path goes even higher, and there's yet another side-path on the right which gives fine views both right, to caves and cliffs, and left, to the great expanse of Watergate Beach (*), which was gleaming white in the sunshine of a winter afternoon when we were last at this spot. After three stiles, the path dips into a gulley for a while, with a Cornish hedge on the left and thick gorse on the right.

3 At the point where the hedge or wall on the left stops, cross the short length of wooden fence. From here the maps show two paths, one straight ahead along the field edge to the nearest gate, from which you turn right on the road, and the other diagonally to the right, crossing two broken-down barbed-wire fences on the way to a pair of gates beside the road; use either path, but the latter cuts out some walking along a road that's busy in summer. (The long, narrow fields marked out by the old fences may be a relic of open-field farming, where the land was divided into many "strips" and shared among a large number of farmers. John Smedley has made a study of the open field system that was operating around the hamlets of Tregurrian and Trevarrian about 150 years ago: see the October 1992 issue of the News Magazine of the Cornwall Association of Local Historians.)

4 Turn left along the minor road almost opposite the pair of gates. Continue past the Tregurrian Camping and Caravanning Club site entrance. At the Watergate Bay Holiday Park entrance, turn right along the road if you want to visit Tregurrian, which has some attractive old cottages and houses; for Trevarrian, turn left along the track. After the gateway, continue ahead beside the hedge on your right for a hundred yards or so, cross the stile on your right and then walk with the hedge on the left to another stile at the far corner of the field - that is, the second corner you come to. From here the path crosses the middle of the field towards the bungalows and then runs along the left side of a short length of hedge to a "stile" - really just a low wooden bar - at the right-hand side of the garden of a newish, pebble-dashed bungalow. Cross the "stile" - you may have to contend with a few nettles and brambles - and continue ahead along a short track to the road. From here, turn right then left for the pub.

WATERGATE BEACH
(AND SOME OTHER PLACE-NAMES)

An alternative name for the beach (used, for example, on the memorial at St Mawgan mentioned in Walk 2) is Tregurrian Beach, but it was called Watergate long before Richard Nixon lent notoriety to the word, and the name is a bit of a mystery. It's quite a common place-name in the south west, but the other examples can more easily be connected with watermill sluice-gates. Other names along the coastal section of this walk, such as Berryl's Point, Griffin's Point, Stem Point and Ontonna Rock, are also unexplained in my books about place-names; some perhaps refer to ships wrecked on them, others to people who lived on or near them. In "Tregurrian" and "Trevarrian", the first syllable means "farm" or "estate", and the rest is probably a version of the original owner's name.

WALK 4
ST COLUMB MINOR, WATERGATE AND TREVELGUE HEAD

About six miles, or can be shortened to about four or three miles.

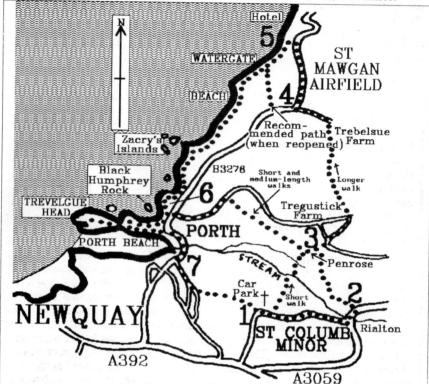

This walk starts at the beautiful church of St Columb Minor, in a setting which retains the atmosphere of a village despite the fact that Newquay has almost absorbed it. The shortest walk brings you fairly directly to Trevelgue Head and Porth. On the longer routes, after a short stretch of attractive country road ending at one of the most historic houses in the area you either follow the valley to the coast or head north through farming country to reach the cliffs above Watergate Beach over a mile further from Newquay, and then follow the coast path to Porth. The quality of this section can be gauged by the fact that it was chosen for the inaugural walk in May 1973 when the opening ceremony of the Cornish Coastal Footpath took place. At low tide it's worth going down to Whipsiderry Beach: the imposing cliffs, rocky islets, caves and ancient mine workings there are fascinating to explore. After walking out to Porth Island (Trevelgue), with its Iron Age fort and wonderful views (arm yourself with binoculars if possible), you return to the church via bungalow-lined roads on the edge of Newquay, and finally a field path. The going is quite easy all the way, but there are a couple of hills to climb, and bare-legged walkers might suffer in a few places. There is some road walking, and one section is likely to be busy with traffic in summer. Shops and pubs are available near Porth beach and at St Columb.

To drive from Newquay, take the main road east (A392). St Columb Minor is signposted to the left about two miles from the centre of Newquay. There is no room for roadside parking near the church, but you will find a car park if you go straight ahead along the narrow road to the left of the church. This is the church car park, so please avoid using it on Sunday mornings, and be prepared to find your car boxed in if there's a wedding or a funeral. The Farmers Arms, next to the church, has a large car park for customers. Best of all, use one of the frequent "Hoppa" buses that run from the centre of Newquay.

ST COLUMB MINOR CHURCH

The church at St Columb Minor is built on a site that appears to have been a sacred place since pre-Christian times. The earliest Christian churches here were probably wooden. A few traces still remain of the first stone church, built about 1100; this was replaced about 150 years later; and finally the present building was begun about 1430. For over 300 years the church boasted a famous rood screen (described in 1685 as "a most curious and costly piece of workmanship, carved and painted with gold, silver, vermillion and bice [pale greenish-blue]; ... a masterpiece of art, in these parts, of that kind") and also some of the best carved bench-ends in Cornwall; but all these were destroyed in a so-called "restoration" in 1795. Nearly a century later, another drastic restoration was carried out; among other things, the nave floor was lowered and the chancel floor raised, burying the bases of the pillars. Despite all this, the interior is attractive and has two interesting slate monuments as well one of the most splendid examples in Cornwall of the Royal Arms presented by Charles II. The tower is the second highest medieval church tower in Cornwall, at 115 feet just a little shorter than that of Probus; for centuries it has acted as a landmark for fishermen. The tower, or at least the pinnacles, can be seen almost all the way round the shorter walk-route. For a brief account of the legend of the church's patron saint, Columba, see the note on Porth in Walk 5.

---

1 The church (*) and its immediate surroundings are well worth exploring. St Columb Minor was a busy market town long before Newquay existed. It was not till 1894 that a separate civil parish of Newquay was created. The Farmers' Arms, almost opposite the church, is a venerable hostelry where, in the days before the church acquired its organ, the church band (flute, clarinet, bass viol and cornopean [cornet]) held its practices for an hour before services. This information comes from the W.I's *Cornwall Villages Book,* where you will also find the story of the fire that destroyed much of the inn in 1913: the Newquay and St Columb Major fire brigades both turned up, and displayed the kind of local "rivalry" (some would call it animosity) so typical of Cornwall by turning their hoses on each other and forgetting the fire.

To start the walk, turn left from the main entrance of the church, along Church Street.

For the shortest route (about three miles), turn left opposite the St Columb Minor Institute. The signed path runs steeply down into the valley and up the far side to Penrose. Just before reaching the main entrance to the converted farm buildings there, take the path on the left with a sign to Trevelgue. Now pick up the directions as given for the medium-length walk (the second part of point 5), starting at line 3.

For the medium-length and longer walks, continue along Church Road, which becomes Priory Road and leads out into the country, with pretty valley views to the left - but please watch out for fast traffic along here. After about half a mile you reach the main Newquay - St Columb Major road, and the large house opposite is Rialton (*). This is not open to the public, but can be seen quite well from the road. (If you cross, please do so with extreme care.) A short way along the lane beside the house is Rialton Mill, records of which go back to 1348; when rebuilt in about 1830 it had two waterwheels, probably both undershot. To continue the walk, turn left as you come from Priory Road, crossing the bridge on the pavement.

2 Immediately beyond the bridge, cross the stile on to the public footpath on the left, signposted to Penrose. The path runs along the valley side, giving fine views of the church, Trevelgue Head beyond the car park, and Towan Head further left. A gate brings you to the beautifully situated Penrose Farm, recently converted as holiday accommodation. Soon you come to a tarmacked drive.

3 *For the medium-length walk, omitting Watergate,* go to the second part of point 5.

For the longer walk: Turn right and continue ahead on the rougher track rather than keeping to the tarmacked surface. Soon you reach a minor road; cross this and walk down the lane opposite to Tregustick Farm. At the road,

---

RIALTON

Old guide books confidently state that there was once an Augustinian priory on this site: hence "Priory Road". In fact Rialton (one of the two Domesday Manors in St Columb Minor parish, the other being Treloy, a little further inland) was never a priory, but by the time of the Domesday survey the ancient Manor was already held by St Petroc's Church, Bodmin, and later it was held jointly by Glasney College, Penryn, and Bodmin Priory. The name (pronounced Rile-ton) is usually explained as meaning "royal manor", but *rial* could refer to ecclesiastical rule: Rialton had jurisdiction over the Hundred of Pydar, one of the six Saxon divisions of Cornwall. A document dated 1283 states, "The Prior of Bomyne has gallows in his Manor of Ryelton." It held its own court and had a dungeon for debtors. The best-known person to live at Rialton was Prior Thomas Vyvyan or Vivian of Bodmin, who in his time was by far the wealthiest and most powerful churchman in Cornwall: "a sort of local Wolsey", as A.L.Rowse puts it. He rebuilt the house between 1508 and 1533; despite a serious fire during the 18th century, parts of the Tudor building remain, notably the porch. A detailed description of the house was included by Charles Henderson in his notes on Cornish parishes (1910-24): see the Journal of the RIC, 1955. Rialton now belongs to the Duchy of Cornwall. In the garden is a holy well inside a pretty and lovingly preserved well-house.

The path near Penrose, showing the effects of salt-laden westerly winds

turn right, and go through the gate marked Trebelsue Farm. (The name is pronounced "Treble-sue" or "Treble-zue" - unusually, with the stress at the start. The old manor of Trebelsue, Trevelsew or Trebiljew belonged to the Arundells [see the note on St Mawgan, Walk 2], and an ancient chapel and burial ground were on the estate: several graves were discovered when a field was being ploughed in 1921.) Continue along this lane for about half a mile, passing the farm and other buildings. At the edge of St Mawgan airfield (*), turn left, and this brings you to the coast road running north from Newquay.

4 Turn right on the road. *(But just as I was preparing this edition for the printer I learned that a long-disused footpath which starts a little way to the left is due to be re-opened by the beginning of 1993. I have indicated it on my map. If this path is now usable there will be a stile at the start of it, and possibly a footpath sign. Using this route would considerably reduce the amount of walking you need to do along a road which is often busy. Whichever way you turn, please go carefully, and walk facing the oncoming traffic.)* After about half a mile (assuming that you turned right on reaching the road), the road begins to descend towards the Watergate Bay Hotel; before you reach the hairpin bend, you can cut across the scrubby land on the left and join the coast path.

RAF ST MAWGAN

Shortly before the Second World War, a small civil airport known as Trebelzue was established here, but with the outbreak of war all civil flights stopped, and in 1941 Trebelzue was taken over by the new RAF station at St Eval. Long runways were built, and in 1943 the name RAF St Mawgan was adopted. Until the end of the war the airfield was used by heavy, long-range American bombers. It was then closed for a few years, but in 1951 re-opened as a Maritime Reconnaissance station. As well as helicopters, the station was equipped with Shackletons; in the early 1970s these were replaced by Canberras and Nimrods. In recent years the training facilities have been greatly improved. During 1992, however, the number of military aircraft based there was steadily reduced, until in October with the departure of 42 Squadron the last of the Nimrods left. At the time of writing (December 1992) RAF St Mawgan is, I am told, "in a state of limbo", but early in 1993 it will be transformed into a helicopter base; presumably, though, the availability of long runways will mean that it will still be used by fixed-wing aircraft during major RAF exercises. A School of Combat Survival and Rescue now operates at St Mawgan, and currently a Joint Maritime Communications Centre is being set up. The St Mawgan International Air Day has for many years been a big attraction in early August, but whether it can still continue on the same scale is doubtful. For some time, a section of the airport has been used by Brymon Airways, who operate a daily passenger service to Heathrow, and there are many people who see St Mawgan as the basis for a full-scale civil airport.

5 Turn left, and now comes a fine, high, mostly level clifftop walk back towards Newquay, overlooking the magnificent Watergate Beach. The headlands, coves and rocky islets along here have evocative names whose origin I can only guess at: Creepinghole Point (referring to a cave with a very low entrance?) and Zacry's or Zichory Islands, for example; Sweden Rock and Fruitful Cove may perhaps have been named from ships wrecked nearby. At Fruitful Cove the cliffs start to take on beautiful colours, some rosy-red; and on the cliff-edge above the cove are two prominent prehistoric mounds (barrows or tumuli), where cremated human remains were buried, along with grave-goods such as weapons, pottery and beads; they are probably between 3,000 and 5,000 years old. Further along is Flory island, otherwise called Black Humphrey Rock; I imagine Black Humphrey as a sort of Captain Hook who plied the main in his ship the *Flory,* striking terror in the hearts of honest seamen. Could Zacry have been his First Mate, who forced prisoners to walk the plank? Close by is Dollar Rock, and I'm sure I can weave that into my story..... There is a less colourful, and therefore more probable, explanation of Black Humphrey as having been a hermit who lived in an old mine working out there, but others say he was a smuggler or wrecker. (Steve Hebdige of the Gallery of Old Newquay tells me that he came from Padstow and died in 1807. The following rhyme is said to be by him:

"When the wind's in the east
I to church as soon as priest.
When the wind's in the west
Pray for me among the rest.")

At the foot of the cliffs between Zacry's Islands and Dollar Rock are spectacular caves with names like Cathedral Cavern, Boulder Cavern, The Infernal Regions and Fern Cavern, whose roof is supposedly covered with ferns, though I couldn't see any. Beyond Dollar Rock, near the bridge to Porth Island, was the Banqueting Hall, once 60 feet wide and 200 feet long. Nigel Tangye describes in his book *Glendorgal* the annual concerts, complete with choir, harmonium and an audience of a thousand, that took place in this cavern. After the Tangye family sold Trevelgue to the Newquay Council, "the man from the Ministry arrived with a huge tuning fork some four feet high" and declared the cave unsafe for concerts. Much more recently, cliff falls led some people to conclude that the cave was too great a hazard to visitors, and men from English China Clays dynamited it out of existence in 1987. Many of the caves and cavities in these cliffs are partially or wholly man-made: Neil Pedlar's note on his card showing the Banqueting Hall says "it was hacked from the rocks as an integral part of the Trevelgue Site". Building stone and metallic ores were mined from it and taken up through a hole in the roof by a crane using a pulley system called "whip and derrick", and this is said to be the origin of the name "Whipsiderry". (It is pronounced "<u>Whip</u>-si-<u>derr</u>-y".) Small mine-workings are dotted all over the cliff-faces, and Black Humphrey Rock is riddled with them. Access to the beach is possible at low tide via steep steps down the cliff immediately before the path out to Trevelgue starts; just beside them, on the right towards the bottom, are two deep mine adits which are said to be part of a 19th century mine called Morganna. Walk on from the top of the steps, and very soon you are at the start of the path out to Trevelgue. Now continue with the directions at point 6.

Black Humphrey Rock and Trevelgue

For the medium-length walk: Instead of turning right at the entrance to the Penrose car park, go left and then turn right on to the path running above the valley, following the Public Footpath sign to Trevelgue. After crossing the makeshift stile on the left side of the gate, turn left through the gap and walk parallel with the fence on your right.   According to the article on Porth in *The Cornwall Village Book* (Cornwall Federation of Women's Institutes, 1991), more than 600 trees have been planted recently on the opposite (southern) slopes of this valley by the British Trust for Conservation, "trying to recreate the wooded valley of Porth" through which St Columba fled from her cruel suitor.   Cross the stile on the right of the next gate; go through the gap in a wire fence; and now head just to the right of the large apartment-block on the skyline. Go through the five-bar gate at the field corner (or cross the stile on the right if it has been cleared of vegetation and other barriers), and walk towards the group of cottages beside the road below. (Notice the two well-preserved prehistoric barrows on the hilltop above them.) At the right corner of the field, where there used to be a gap in the barbed wire fence, when I checked this walk in November 1992 there was a new section of fencing, but this was not barbed and was easy to step over. Go through a metal gate at the bottom, and over a bridge. Turn right for a few yards, and then cut across the valley-floor, making for the telegraph pole in front of the cottages, near which there is a footpath sign and a rather awkward stile. At the road, turn left, passing the Whipsiderry Hotel. There are good views over Newquay from here. When you reach the main road, cross to the cliff-edge path. From here at low tide you could go down the steps to Whipsiderry Beach, as described two paragraphs earlier, before walking out to Porth Island and Trevelgue Head (*).

6 I suggest you keep to the right-hand side all the way round the headland (except, of course, where you have to cross the footbridge), thus returning to

---

TREVELGUE HEAD

Say Tre-<u>vel</u>-gy, with a hard g at the end. (The older guide books usually spell the name "Trevelga".) Most locals call it Porth Island. It is reputed to be the finest example in Europe of an Iron Age fortified living site. Excavations have revealed that it was continuously inhabited from about 300BC for at least six centuries, and a post-Roman structure was found suggesting use perhaps until 600 or 700AD. As well as a number of Bronze Age barrows (burial mounds), there are four Iron Age earth ramparts with ditches on the landward side of the chasm, and two more beyond that. "All of these," writes Nigel Tangye, "were faced with huge slabs of stone" until modern builders took them. Remains of hut circles and a field system were also excavated. Finds included sling-stones, glass beads, Roman coins and large amounts of slag from the smelting of metallic ores. Iron was mined from the cliffs on the north side in ancient times as well as more recently. The sea has destroyed much of the original headland, as shown by the fact that there are remains of the ramparts on what is now a rock some fifty yards out. A blow-hole near the tip of the headland provides spectacular displays at half-tide in stormy weather: waves entering a cave on the seaward side are bottled up in it and with explosive booms force spray through narrow fissures.

the road close to Porth Beach. Turn right there, past a group of shops and cafés and a pub, The Mermaid. The bridge carrying the road over the Porth River dates only from 1902; until then a ford provided the only way across.

7 Take the first turning left, Lewarne Road, which goes fairly steeply uphill. Near the top, turn left on to Lewarne Crescent, and a few yards later take the Public Footpath on the left, signposted to St Columb Minor Church. After a gate, the path runs just to the left of the nearest electricity supply pole. After the next gate go straight ahead, keeping left of the hedge. This brings you to the lane to the church.

The Fern Cavern, Whipsiderry Beach

WALK 5
NEWQUAY ITSELF:
A BEACH AND SEAFRONT WALK

About three miles

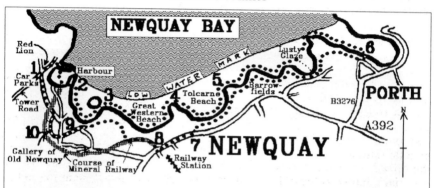

Obviously, you don't need many directions to enable you to walk along the Newquay cliffs and beaches, so my main purpose here is to help you notice the interesting details and to provide some historical background. Careful timing is important: check the time of low water and aim to reach the north-east end of the beach (Lusty Glaze and Porth) then; in other words, if you do the walk exactly according to my directions, start about an hour before low water - or a little earlier to allow ample time for exploration of caves and other features. Ideally, pick a day when low water is particularly low (say, 0.5 metres or less), because otherwise you may not be able to get past the headland between Lusty Glaze and Porth beach; even when the tide is very low, a little paddling may be necessary there. (Details of tide times and heights can be got from local papers and booklets available at most newsagents, or by enquiring at the Tourist Information Centre.) If you have a copy of "Newquay's Pictorial Past", published by the Newquay Old Cornwall Society, I suggest you take it with you, because it's fascinating to compare the old photographs with the scene as it is. In what follows I shall occasionally refer to particular pages, in this form: NPP 4, NPP 16, etc. The first edition of that book is now out of print, but plans are well advanced for a slightly revised new edition to be published by Landfall in association with the OCS. In addition, you can see most of the pictures at the Gallery of Old Newquay, and I have included directions to that in point 9. The walk is full of beauty, interest and contrast at any time of year, but best of all out of season if you're lucky enough to be here then. The going is easy throughout, and you are never very far from refreshments and public toilets, even during the winter. Particularly handily placed at the start and end of the route is the Red Lion. Though large, it has a cosy atmosphere; the views from it are stupendous, the service is friendly and quick, and I particularly recommend the macaroni cheese. (In case you're wondering - no, I'm not a shareholder in the company, nor do I accept bribes. Not so far, at least....)

If you need to park your car first, I recommend the two car parks at the harbour end of Tower Road; see the start of Walk 6. From there walk down Tower Road to the Red Lion at the roundabout. If you are ·approaching on foot from the town centre, come along Fore Street: the Red Lion is at the far end of it. (Shortly before you reach it, it's worth turning left to look at the old alleyway named Deer Park, where a few old cottages have survived - a relic of the fishing village Newquay once was.)

1 From the pub, go down North Quay Hill, which gives you a fine view over the harbour(*) and bay. Bear right on to North Quay and go down the steep steps on to the beach. Take care here, especially on the slippery rocks. Walk past the small quay, now stranded at the centre of the harbour, and up the slipway to the Harbour Mission and the modern lifeboat house, where at certain times you can see the boat and records of the rescues carried out since 1864. From there I suggest you go out on to the south pier; on the Harbourmaster's building is a plaque about the history of the harbour and mineral railway. Walk back to the Aquarium, which is built into the mouth of the railway tunnel; it's worth going in to inspect the photographs and other material relating to the old mineral railway, even if you don't want to see the fish. Continue past the chandlery and down the steps on to Towan Beach.

2 Although it's pleasant to stroll by the water's edge, I shall assume you are keeping close to the cliffs all the way along. The coastline is deeply indented with inlets, coves and caves, and almost immediately on your right there is a good example of a sea-wall built to prevent, or at least delay, the sea's undermining of the cliff. Some of the holes in the cliffs were made by miners; for example, in 1838 the Newquay Silver and Lead Mine at Mount Wise had its adit (drainage shaft) discharging water behind what was when I originally researched this book in 1989 the Cosy Nook Theatre. That stood in what is now (November 1992) a yawning gap on Towan Promenade, on the left side of the "Panorama Caferteria" *(sic)*. The water still flowed from the adit when Hamilton Jenkin wrote Vol VII of *Mines and Miners of Cornwall* in 1963, and presumably it does so now. (Perhaps the large silvery drainpipe emerging from the cliff carries it.) To me, one of the most intriguing things about walking below cliffs in old mining areas is to try to work out which of the caves, crevices and streams are natural and which man-made. According to Barry Atkinson's *Mining Sites in Cornwall and South West Devon* (Truran, 1988) the cliffs further along, beyond Tolcarne Point, "are, in some places, honeycombed with the old men's levels and adits of several ancient mines that prospected the area for copper and lead during the years 1830-1870." ("Old men" refers to miners working before official records began to be kept.) I must admit that I wasn't convinced I could detect any of these, but see what you can find. For details about these mines, look up Tolcarne, Wheal Narrow and Rosecliff in Hamilton Jenkin's book. While still on Towan Beach, compare the scene with *NPP* pages 4-8: Towan Promenade was once occupied by a large fish cellar, the Speculation, with Treffry and Unity cellars close by (see the boxed note on Newquay's Fish Cellars in Walk 6); later came the Mineral Water factory and the Steam Laundry plus public baths, opened in 1895 - all of which presumably made full use of the supply of good fresh water from the old mine adit; later still the Cosy Nook in the form of a

NEWQUAY HARBOUR

A small harbour existed here by 1396, but storms destroyed it. In 1439, the Bishop of Exeter gave leave for another harbour to be built, and the Tudor historian Richard Carew refers to "Newe Kaye, a place on the north coast, so called, because in former times the neighbours attempted to supplie the defect of nature by art in making there a kay for the road of shipping." In 1615 a new pier was built. By 1775 there were still only a dozen cottages nearby. In 1825 the Manor of Towan Blistra, which included the harbour and hamlet, was bought by a Londoner, Richard Lomax, and he started work on the south pier. Soon afterwards, the harbour attracted the attention of the great industrialist, Joseph Thomas Austen, who needed a port on the north coast, in addition to Par on the south, to serve his mines and china clay works. He built a new north pier in 1841, having bought most of the manor and changed his surname to Treffry (pronounced to rhyme with "reply") in 1838. Even so, much of the activity here till the last quarter of the 19th century would have been related to fishing, especially during the latter part of that time, when huge catches of pilchards were made. Before the start of this century, vast shoals of pilchards were becoming rare. For an interesting discussion of the reasons for this, see Richard Pearse's *The Land beside the Celtic Sea* (Truran, 1983). One of his suggestions is that the coming of the main-line railway to Cornwall in 1859 led to a great increase in the consumption of Cornish crabs "up-country", and crab larvae are an important part of the

diet of pilchards. By a neat irony, that same railway also helped to save Newquay by bringing shoals of holidaymakers to replace the fishy ones, and also by increasing the trade in minerals to the harbour. Already by February 1849, Treffry had built a line for use by horse-drawn wagons to Newquay from the great lead mine of East Wheal Rose near St Newlyn East (see Walk 1 in *A View from St Agnes Beacon),* and bored a tunnel 240 feet long (288 feet according to John Vaughan) at an incline of 1 : 4.5 so that wagons could be raised and lowered by cables between the cliff-top and the south pier. A line known as the Tram Track ran from the cliff-top to the present site of the station: on my map I have given a rough indication of its course. In 1872, when the harbour was at its busiest, a jetty was added in the middle of the harbour, and wooden trestles carried rails out on to that. *NPP* 9-13 show most of these features of the harbour, and on pages 38-9 are pictures of the tunnel and the steam engines that operated the cables after the original horse-whim fell out of use. Like other north coast harbours, Newquay's was always at a disadvantage compared with the more sheltered ones in the south; and when steam ships came into use early in this century Newquay harbour was too small for them. The last loads of coal and china clay were handled in 1921, the last load of herrings in 1926, and the Tram Track was used for the last time in 1931. The wooden bridge out to the central jetty was demolished early in the 1950s.

distinctly un-cosy-looking tent. If planning permission is given, the Cosy Nook site may next be occupied by an aquarium, much more "up-market" than the one in the old railway tunnel. Page 6 in *NPP* shows the Island (*) before the building of the suspension bridge.

THE ISLAND

According to *NPP* it was "formerly known as Jago's Island where chickens were kept". Mr Peter Cocks, who lives on it now, calls it Towan Island in an article he wrote about it for the free "Welcome to Newquay" publication (1992). He does not mention the chickens, but says it was once a potato patch. The famous suspension bridge is, he says, four feet wide and a hundred long, and was built ninety years ago. At first a fee of 2d was charged to cross the bridge to a tea house on the Island; then in 1906 a Mr O'Flaherty built the first bungalow. At the end of World War I that was bought by Sir Oliver Lodge, a spiritualist whose séances were attended by Sir Athur Conan Doyle, the creator of Sherlock Holmes. For over ten years, writes Mr Cocks, the building on the Island was an art gallery, but he does not give the dates of this. He says the Island is much more comfortable to live on than it looks, partly because of the shelter provided by tamarisks.

3 Pass under the bridge now to Great Western Beach (named from the nearby railway; previously it was called Bothwith's Beach), and walk round by the black cliffs here to Bishop's Rock, which does look rather like a bishop's mitre. There are deep, narrow caves close to it, and on the far side of the beach is a double cave; notice the multicoloured rocks in the wider cave. One of the hotels overlooking Great Western Beach is the Victoria, which in my 1922 "Homeland" guidebook claimed to be the "Finest Hotel in England", and somewhat less controversially the "Only Hotel in England with Lift from every floor to Bathing Beaches". The lift is still in working order and offers what the Hotel now advertises as "A unique experience."

4 Beyond the next headland is Tolcarne Beach (compare *NPP* 49), and immediately on the right here, near the top of the cliff, is an adit from Rosecliff Mine; the drainpipe was perhaps put there to avoid splashing sunbathers below. Past the garish beach-hut development is, in contrast, a particularly beautiful cave, with lovely colours again and ferns growing in tiny crevices among the 45°-angled strata. Standing here, it's easy to imagine the violent forces that created this scene millions of years ago.

5 Several more good caves and contorted rock formations follow as you walk round and beyond Crigga Rocks. This name probably refers to the ancient burial mounds on the Barrowfields above. Soon you are at Lusty Glaze - a delightful, mystifying name. Some early guide books call it "Lystra Glaze", which tempts me to suggest a connection with the village that once existed where Newquay now stands: Towan Blistra. "Listri" was Cornish for "boats"; "glas" meant "green, blue, grey" and was sometimes used to refer to the sea ... so perhaps you'd like to try your hand at coining a picturesque translation of "Lusty Glaze". Just to the left of the platform for bathing huts and other amenities, you may be able to see a slanting groove or channel in the cliff face. This was cut in 1775 to enable skips containing sand, seaweed and coal to be drawn up by ropes to the top, there to be loaded on to barges on John Edyvean's canal - or perhaps it would be more correct to say, one of his two canals (see Walk 1); some say that china clay was lowered down the incline, but Mr Roger Lacy, who has made a close study of the history of this area, thinks that unlikely, since the canal never reached the china clay region. Past the next headland is Porth Beach; walk, paddle or wade round to it if you're happy to do so. (If not, there is a safe path up to the cliff-top behind the holiday development, so you don't need to scale the precarious-looking steps near the headland. At the top, turn left if you want to include Porth in the walk.) "Wine Cove" at the headland implies smuggling activities; so, too, does "The Great Cupboard", a slightly larger inlet on the Porth side. The big house on the top here, built probably about 1850 and converted into a hotel a century later, is Glendorgal, lovingly described by its owner, Nigel Tangye, in his little book of the same name. *NPP* 57 shows Porth Beach as it once was. Gradually the cliffs get lower, and there are two flights of steps to the top, but I suggest you continue through the beach car park, up to the road (toilets here) and then to the Post Office/Stores. Few Cornish places can have been more drastically changed by the holiday trade than Porth (*): *NPP* 56 will illustrate what I mean; yet somehow this little bit of it has retained the atmosphere of a village, at least when visited out of season. Mr Whale at the shop showed me where Porth's fish cellar, Concord, probably was (behind

*The schooner "Johann Carl" unloading coal on Porth beach.
The photograph is undated, but must be between 1899, when she was
bought by Alexander Stephens of Porth, and 1917, when she sank.*

PORTH

Its original name was St Columb Porth: the Irish Saint Columba is supposed to have landed here when fleeing from a pagan prince her father had tried to force her to marry. Old maps show that there was once a forest where the beach now is; on the other hand, seashells have been found well up the valley at Rialton (see Walk 4), so there must have been several big changes in the levels of sea and land. St Columba, according to the legend, fled through the forest but was finally caught and beheaded; her blood was transformed into the stream which now feeds the Porth reservoir (Walk 10) and reaches the sea at Porth. Although hardly a sheltered haven, Porth was used as a harbour for cargo and fishing vessels from ancient times, when local iron and other minerals were traded, until early this century, when ships carrying coal would come in on a high tide and unload on the beach.

the shop, near a cottage called Concord, originally the store for nets and salt), and pointed out an old mooring ring in the wall almost opposite the shop, a survival from the time when the road ran straight down to the beach here. A limekiln used to stand at the top of the beach, close to where the shop is now. Also close by was a coalyard, supplied by ships like the one in the old photograph. Shipbuilding once thrived at Porth, but the last ship of any size launched here was the *Lady Jane,* in 1880. Porth's oldest cottage, Gwenna, dates from around 1600; near the shop is Morvah, originally a farmhouse (c. 1660).

6 At the start of the walk back to Newquay along the cliff-top, the South West Way acorn signs direct you round past the entrance to Glendorgal (this area is called Greensplat, meaning green plot of land), above Lusty Glaze, and then across or around the delightful area, like a well-kept golf course without the lethal missiles, called Barrowfields (*). The promenade that comes next is Narrowcliff; compare *NPP* 50 and 51.

BARROWFIELDS

Once there were at least eighteen Bronze Age (c. 2000 to 1500 BC) burial mounds here, but in 1821 all except three were destroyed, and even they are poorly preserved. Round barrows are common in Cornwall; usually they were built on ridges, hills and clifftops with panoramic views. It seems that the corpse was cremated, at least in later times, and then earth, turf and surface stones were piled on top. Borlase, writing in 1754, envisaged large gangs scooping up material: "The Earth was brought and pour'd out of the Helmets..." The conical or bowl-like mounds have, for the most part, withstood the battering of the elements very well, and since little if any useful building-stone was included, men (apart from archaeologists and "developers") have usually left them alone.

---

7 When you reach the Rocklands Hotel, you have to walk along the main road (Cliff Road) for a while. On the left soon is the railway station. *NPP* 44, 45 and probably 46 show Cliff Road "in the old days".

8 Soon after passing the station, turn right from the main road on to the signposted Public Footpath, which follows the course of the old mineral railway. Climb the steps at the bridge, go to the end of Bridge Road, turn left (Trebarwith Crescent) and first right (Island Crescent), and take the path across Killacourt Green above The Island and Towan Beach. Continue past the Cliffside Hotel and follow the road, turning right past the entrance to the Camelot Cinema.

9 *Now I'll direct you to the Gallery of Old Newquay, an excellent small museum of local history: I hope that my brief notes have whetted your appetite for much greater detail. The exhibits will tell you a lot, and the people who give up their time to run the museum are always pleased to answer questions if they can. The Gallery opens from 10 till 4 Monday to Friday between Easter and 30th September; in April, Monday to Friday afternoons only; and in winter just on Wednesdays.*
From the Camelot, turn left, fork right (Beach Road), cross the main road (Fore Street) and continue ahead up Chapel Hill. The Gallery is on the left at

the corner, next to the old chapel. Eventually it is planned that the chapel building itself will house the museum: work was under way as I was preparing this new edition.

10 To return to the Red Lion, continue to the end of Chapel Hill. Ahead is Gateways supermarket, beside the Whim Car Park, so called because the two steam engines were here that raised and lowered the wagons in the tunnel down to the harbour. (See *NPP* 38.) Go right, down to Fore Street, and turn left. The Red Lion is at the end. The exterior of the pub hasn't changed much since the 1920s, to judge by old postcards still on sale, but *NPP* 17 shows how different it was as Prout's Hotel.

Railway wagons loaded with coal and pipes at the foot of the tunnel, Newquay harbour (Photograph kindly supplied by Joyce Greenham)

WALK 6

NEWQUAY, THE GANNEL, PENTIRE POINT EAST AND TOWAN HEAD

One walk of about seven miles,
plus details of three shorter versions.
See note at end for details of shorter routes.

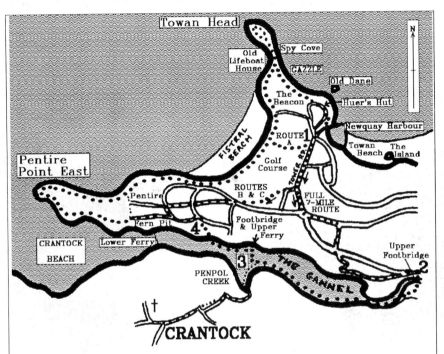

IMPORTANT: *For the walk along the Gannel you need to avoid high tide (though I'm told it's usually negotiable except at the highest springs), and in order to cross the footbridge near Penpol Creek you must be there within a couple of hours of low water; otherwise you will have to use one of the two ferry services, and these operate only from early June to mid-September. The footbridge is about an hour's walk from Tower Road by this route.*

This is a splendid walk, full of variety and interest, and even the longest version could hardly be called strenuous. You are close to built-up areas all the time, so toilets and refreshments are available at several points, at least in season; and yet on the upper part of the Gannel and out on the headlands you can feel a long way from "civilisation". There was no Gannel Link Road when I first researched this route; now that it is in place, if you do the full seven-mile walk you are faced with the need to cross it at a point where there is (or was, in September 1992) no assistance for pedestrians, and to walk at the side of it for a few yards. This is regrettable, but at present I can see no practicable alternative. Even at low tide waterproof footwear is advisable when walking beside the Gannel. Photographs in Newquay's Pictorial Past *(see details under Walk 5) are referred to where I have indicated NPP.*

Directions are given from the two car parks on Tower Road, Newquay, near the junction with Fore Street.

1 For the full seven-mile route, walk back from the car park to Tower Road and turn right, past the Tower, built in 1835 as a gentleman's holiday residence, and now the home of Newquay Golf Club. Where Atlantic Road and Crantock Street cross, continue ahead up Higher Tower Road. Turn left at the T-junction (Mount Wise), then first right on to Tregunnel Hill, passing the Fire Station. Cross the new main road with extreme care and go a few yards to the left, where Tregunnel Hill continues, a tiny country lane which feels like - and indeed is - a survivor from another age. It curves left, passing Tregunnel House (presumably a relic of the farm that once worked this land), becomes Gannel Road and runs beside the river; in fact, at high water during spring tides it's in the river rather than beside it. A sign at the entrance to one of the ugly modern blocks along here reads "Tides Reach En Suite Rooms" - and it could be true! Inexorably you are brought back to the Link Road; luckily there is a pavement. Continue in the same direction along that.

2 As you approach the boating lake at Trenance, you will see a footbridge across the Gannel (*) - provided, of course, that it's not under water. Go over the bridge and turn right on the wide track that runs below the low cliff. (For comments on some details connected with this part of the walk, see Section 2 in Walk 7.) You are likely to find several muddy patches, especially soon after high tide (and if it's too bad there is a path along the other side of

Penpol Creek

the river which I'm told is usually drier: see the italicised note in the same section of Walk 7); but the nearer the sea you get the sandier the track becomes, and by the time you reach Penpol Creek you are on a beach and perhaps surrounded by sunbathing holidaymakers.

THE GANNEL

In 1987, when a new housing estate was built on the site of a medieval farm at Trethellan on the slopes leading down to the north shore of the Gannel, a labourer during his lunch break happened to notice some "primitive looking" chunks of crude pottery. His find led to the unearthing of the best-preserved remains of a Bronze Age village yet discovered in Cornwall, and an Iron Age cemetery. A very detailed report of the results of the "dig" carried out in the summer of that year can be found in *Cornish Archaeology* No. 30 (1991). An Iron Age hill fort known as Treringey Round, overlooking the Gannel on the south side (see Walk 7), provides further evidence of early habitation - and there were in fact several other such "rounds" nearby, of which little obvious evidence now survives. In *Old Cornish Bridges and Streams* (1928), Charles Henderson writes, "In the middle ages, before the sand had choked it, the Gannel was a port, carrying on a brisk trade with Wales and Ireland. Even in the 18th century Welsh coal for the Truro smelting works was unshipped at Penpoll or Trevemper and carried across Cornwall by a pack-horse way that can still be traced..... Trevemper Bridge is now the limit of the tide..... It was rebuilt with one arch in the last century." The old bridge is still preserved, beside the main road about half a mile south of the first footbridge you cross on this walk. In *Old Newquay,* Miss Husband tells about the ships that used to discharge their cargoes just below the Fern Pit, where the lower ferry runs, to be conveyed from there to Trevemper and Crantock. There was a boat-building yard at the foot of Tregunnel Hill, and in the winter any boats from Newquay that were not in use would be brought round there to sheltered moorings. A little downriver from Tregunnel (at Trethellan, in fact, where the Bronze Age settlement was) a lead mine called Chiverton Wheal Rose operated until 1864, and further still down-river on the Crantock side was a lead-and-silver-smelting works. (Silver and lead are often found together, and there was a small enterprise called the Newquay Silver and Lead Mine operating till about 1845 nearby, in the Mount Wise area.) Iron ore from the Great Perran Iron Lode (see *A View from St Agnes Beacon,* Walk 4) was brought to the Gannel for shipment to Wales. Miss Husband writes, too, of the Gannel Crake - perhaps an exotic bird, but no known species, surely, could strike such terror into all that hear its cry. "It was like nothing I have ever heard before," said one man. "It was like a thousand voices in pent-up misery with one long drawn wail dying away in the distance." What surprises me most about the Gannel Crake is that Newquay doesn't seem to have milked it as a tourist attraction - a kind of Cornish Loch Ness Monster. The name, "Gannel", by the way, comes from the English word "channel" or "kennel", a gutter or drain. Any suggestion that the Crake is actually the Gannel laughing like a drain at gullible human beings should be treated with the contempt it deserves.

The Gannel in August 1989

(From here you could visit Crantock by going to the head of the creek, crossing the stream by means of the stepping stones or the bridge, and walking up the lane. After about a quarter of a mile, follow the footpath sign to Crantock on the right, crossing two stiles and re-joining the road beside the wayside cross of St Crantock ["restored upon its ancient base A.S. 1928" - and, in case you're wondering, A.S. stands for anno salutis, "in the year of salvation"]. The road ahead brings you to the centre of the village. This diversion into Crantock would add about a mile to the walk. For a note on Crantock, see Walk 8.)

3 If the tide is too high for you to cross the footbridge over the Gannel opposite Penpol Creek, use the rowing-boat ferry (unless, of course, you're walking "out of season"). On the Newquay side, go left along the foreshore until you reach a sea wall with a red-and-white "chessboard" pattern. Just past this, follow the Public Footpath sign, up steps at first.

4 At the road (Pentire Crescent), turn left, then left again on to Riverside Avenue; at the corner (Fistral Crescent) continue straight ahead. Now you have a good view left of Crantock beach and church; look back for a panorama of the Gannel, worth comparing with *NPP* 27. From Riverside Crescent you can see the spire of Cubert church, and St Agnes Beacon on the skyline. Soon you pass the Fern Pit Café and the path down to the other ferry. When the road ends, continue ahead along the path across The Warren to Pentire Point East, which, like almost every other headland along this stretch of coast, bears evidence of habitation in ancient times: notice the two barrows (burial mounds) near the track, which may be anything from 3,000 to 4,000 years old. At the Point itself is a small quarry; the path continues on the landward side of that, and there is a fine view from the top of the ridge across Fistral Bay to Towan Head and ten miles past that to Trevose Head near Padstow. Soon after rounding the headland you will come to a couple of small inlets called Lewinnick ("Fox"?) Cove and Swimming Cove. Here a private road leads down to a surprisingly grand and ornate piece of architecture named on the maps as Lewinnick Lodge but popularly known hereabouts as "Baker's Folly". I'm told that Mr Baker was a millionaire who, having travelled the world, built this in 1934-5 as his retirement home. He has become almost a legendary figure, and there may be no more truth in the tales told about him nowadays than in those of the Cornish giants and piskies. According to one version I have heard, when he was 80 his wife died and he married his secretary; another story has it that he built Lewinnick Lodge for his wife and planned to build a similar mansion on the other side of the headland for his mistress, with a tunnel to link the two! He died, it would seem, before this plan could be fulfilled. Yet another version is that he was abroad when the house was built, and the builders put it on the wrong side of the headland - the shady rather than the sunny side. What does appear to be plain fact is that in its early years the Lodge was the venue for grand balls and other lavish social events; and that after a period of neglect it is now divided into residential flats. The coastal path round Fistral Bay (*) is too obvious to require directions from me; for much of the way it

---

FISTRAL BAY

Late in 1989, tiny bone fragments from a "Giant Irish Elk" or deer estimated to have lived between 65 and 80 thousand years ago were discovered in the cliff face by a beach attendant who was clearing up litter. The bones were apparently six feet up the cliff face, showing how much higher the beach was when the animal lived. The deer was about eight feet high to the shoulder and its antlers were ten feet across, according to a natural history expert. Rather more recent but now equally extinct was North Wheal Providence, a lead mine whose workings were beneath what is now the golf course. *NPP* has an old picture of Fistral on page 24.

---

runs along the edge of the golf course (not a very attractive stretch, and if the tide is low enough I'd recommend using the beach), and then the path to the left of the Headland Hotel (*) leads out towards Towan Head. ("Towan" means sand-dune, and the first syllable rhymes with "how" rather than with "low".) Beside the car park is the Old Lifeboat House (*), and close by is the slipway at Spy Cove - at a gradient of one in two-and-a-quarter the steepest lifeboat slip in Britain. Launchings were spectacular, and crowds used to gather to watch practice runs - usually done on August Bank Holiday. See *NPP* 22 and 23. For another aspect of the history of this spot, see the boxed note about the Harbour of Refuge. The viewpoint above the toilets marks the site of the chimney of the lime-kiln mentioned in that note. Continue to Towan Head. The concrete structures there are the remains of a World War I signal and searchlight station. The picturesque Look-Out House was built in 1921 as a consolation for the destruction of the old one which stood on the

THE HEADLAND HOTEL

This was the second large hotel to be built in Newquay, opening in 1900. The entrepreneur responsible, Silvanus Trevail, had built the Atlantic Hotel eight years earlier. Several books - notably David Mudd's *Cornwall in Uproar* (Bossiney) and Donald Bray's *Stories of the North Cornish Coast* (Truran) - tell the surprising story of "The Headland Riots", in which townspeople, resentful of the threat posed by these developments to public access to Towan headland, held a Dutch auction of builders' materials and a workman's hut and cast them into the sea. When Trevail visited Newquay he was jeered and pelted with eggs and every other available missile. The local council withdrew planning permission for the new hotel on the grounds of faulty drains, but reversed its decision six months later when the fuss had died down. Edward Duke of Cornwall, the future King Edward VIII, attracted largely by the closeness of a good golf course, stayed at the Headland frequently for several years from 1911 onwards; as Donald Bray says, "he put Newquay on the map as surely as his Georgian Great-Great-Uncle had publicised Brighton."

THE OLD LIFEBOAT HOUSE

In *Old Newquay* you can read about the excitement in the town in 1860 when "Georgie Burt's six great horses" brought the wagon bearing the town's first purpose-built lifeboat, *Joshua,* to the house built for her on Fore Street. She had to be taken down the hill to the harbour for launching. Later lifeboats were too big for that, so in 1895 a new slip was built on the headland, and later a house for the boat; these continued in use till 1934. When the lifeboat returned from an outing she was mounted on a trolley and hauled through the streets back to the headland by a team of eight horses. A good photograph showing this procedure in action is in Fisher Barham's *Ships and Shores around Old Cornwall* (Glasney Press, 1982); the same picture is in Joan Rendell's *North Cornwall in the Old Days* (Bossiney, 1983), but Miss Rendell's caption states that it shows the lifeboat being launched. A shortage of horses is said to have been the reason for the closure of the lifeboat service in 1934. Further details about the Newquay lifeboats, and other aspects of local history, can be read on the excellent green plaques set up by the local council here and at other strategic points such as the harbour. From the modern lifeboat house at the harbour you can buy the latest Yearbook, which includes photographs of the early and modern Newquay lifeboats and a history of their work.

Beacon, where the War Memorial near the Atlantic Hotel is now. The clifftop path from Towan Head to Newquay overlooks various small coves and impressive caves, one group of which are called the Tea Caverns, a reflection of their former use by smugglers. Many if not all these caverns owe their origin to early mining activity. The rocky outcrop off the next small headland is known as the Old Dane, and the bay between that and Towan Head is the Gazzle, from a Cornish word meaning armpit and therefore a recess or inlet. For a short distance the coast path consists of a road (King Edward Crescent), and beside this is the Huer's Hut (*). From there, follow

Directions continue on page 55.

THE HARBOUR OF REFUGE

Perhaps the most important contribution to Newquay's history by any one person was that of Joseph Thomas Treffry; for the main note about him see "Newquay Harbour" (Walk 5), and there is more in a note on Walk 9. His fertile mind devised many schemes; one of the last and most ambitious was for a harbour on the west side of Towan headland to provide shelter for ships when storms battered Newquay Bay. The idea was to cut a channel across the isthmus at the narrowest point, very near the lifeboat house; this work was in fact carried out, and for many years people had to use a bridge if they wanted to walk out to the tip of the headland. In 1848-9 foundations for harbour walls were laid and one pier was completed. A lime kiln built on the site of the old Spy fish cellar is sometimes said to have been constructed specifically to provide lime for the mortar Treffry's project required. In 1923 Miss Husband wrote about her childhood memories of the work in progress: "The huge blocks of granite were brought from Luxulyan by the then new railway to the Newquay Harbour and were shipped on flat-bottomed boats. These were rowed across the Gazel to the rocks and the granite was then hoisted into the waggons by a derrick which had been erected on a staging." Men then pushed the waggons along a line across to where the harbour was being built. In 1850 Treffry died, and the project died with him.

NEWQUAY FISH CELLARS

During the heyday of Newquay's prosperity as a fishing port, various companies owned seine boats and fish curing cellars. (Seining is a method of fishing using a heavy, fine-meshed net about 1,000 feet [305m.] long and 70 feet [21m.] wide; lead weights are attached to one long edge and cork floats to the opposite one. The techniques of seining and of preparing the pilchards for sale in the cellars are vividly described by S. Teague Husband. A typical cellar was able to handle about 500 hogsheads, each containing some 3,000 salted pilchards, packed so tightly that levers with heavy weights on the end had to be used to force them in.) By 1831 there were seven cellars, and later more. Their names were: Spy (the oldest), Fly, Good Intent, Active, Toby, Rose, Unity, Speculation, Hope, Treffry or "Flour and Fat", Concord (at Porth), Union and Point. The Newquay seiners made many spectacular catches, such as the one described by Cyril Noall: "On October 17 1863, a huge mass of fish was seen to fill the bay from Towan to Trevelgue Heads. During the following week the concerns took fish to the value of £20,000, and over 1,000 fish carts came to the town from all parts of the county. This was said to have been the greatest catch of fish ever made on the north coast." *(Cornish Seines and Seiners)* Noall points out that the wide beaches of Newquay were in one way ideal for seining, but also led to severe damage to the seines in stormy weather. The last large catch of pilchards at Newquay was in 1893. All the cellar buildings have gone now: the last to be demolished (in 1989) was Toby, near the Tower Road car parks. Some are recalled in names, such as Hope Terrace, The Active Seine Shelter and Fly Promenade (both above the harbour), Spy Cove and Concord Cottage. Photographs of some cellars have survived: see *NPP* 5 and 14, for example.

THE HUER'S HUT

The Newquay Old Cornwall Society believes this may date from the 14th century and originally have been a hermitage with a light to guide shipping. A Cornwall Archaeological Society Field Guide of 1962 says the chimney is "late medieval". An old document records, "1838, restored by Vivian, paid in fish". From the late 18th to the early 20th centuries such huts - often known as "baulking houses" - were used by the "huers" employed by the seine companies to watch for pilchard shoals and alert the fishermen. According to Cyril Noall in *Cornish Seines and Seiners,* "Warning of approaching shoals was given here, most unusually, by a bell." Miss Husband, however, tells how "Each huer, with his megaphone-like trumpet, which was longer than a coach horn, shouted *Heva, Heva. The Cry is up* and *The Cry is up* ..... As the shouts were echoed from cliff to cliff, from St Columb Minor to Crantock, a frantic rush was made by all concerned .... " For further details about the huers and this building see the "Newquay Town Trail Walkabout". A splendid old photograph of the huers is in *NPP* (page 18).

the acorn signs, which lead you along the cliff above Fly Cove and past "The Active Seine Shelter". (For an explanation of this, together with Spy and Fly, see the note on Newquay's Fish Cellars.) To return to the suggested starting point, continue along the road above the harbour (North Quay Hill), and at the roundabout cross to Tower Road.

SHORTER ROUTES

A   TOWAN HEAD ONLY *(About two miles)*

Take the footpath which runs between the two car parks. It starts at a wooden farm gate with a stone stile to the left, and then crosses the golf links. Beware of small round missiles. It brings you to the coastal footpath running above Fistral Beach; turn right, and now follow the main route as described in the final 30-or-so lines.

B   PENTIRE POINT EAST ONLY *(Nearly four miles)*
C   PENTIRE POINT EAST AND TOWAN HEAD
(About five and a half miles)

Follow the main directions as far as Atlantic Road; there turn right, and at the left bend a few yards later join the path in front of you, which runs left for a few yards and then follows the golf course perimeter fence. Before long, Pentire Road is on your left. At the end of the path, go along Pentire Avenue (between the two hotels) and take the second left turning, Pentire Crescent, then turn right on to Riverside Avenue. Now continue ahead, as described near the start of part 4 of the main directions. For walk C, continue to the end of the main directions; for walk B, take the official coast path beside the tall golf-course fence at Fistral, and turn right at the one gap in it. The path across the golf course leads to the two Tower Road car parks.

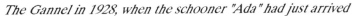

The Gannel in 1928, when the schooner "Ada" had just arrived

WALK 7
About five miles

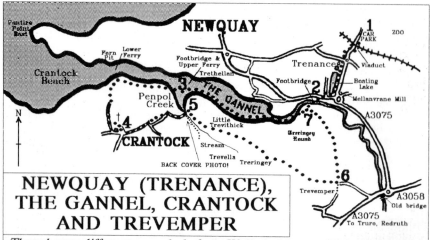

NEWQUAY (TRENANCE), THE GANNEL, CRANTOCK AND TREVEMPER

Though very different as a whole from Walk 6, this one shares a mile or so of the same route beside the Gannel and would be affected in the same way by high tides. It is quite an easy walk, and nicely varied. The delights of the Gannel estuary and of Crantock are celebrated elsewhere in this book; the Trenance area is one of the most attractive parts of Newquay, and the walk from Penpol back to Trenance via Trevemper gives long views, especially to the south and east. There are toilets, various seasonal shops and cafés and the Gannel Inn, close to the suggested start/end point of this walk; Crantock, which is roughly half-way, has a choice of seasonal and all-year shops and pubs, plus toilets.

Roadside parking is sometimes available near the boating lake at Trenance, either on Trenance Lane to the west side of it or on the main road (Trevemper Road) to the east. Failing those, I suggest you use the long-stay car park at Trenance Gardens, near Newquay Zoo. For that, continue north along Trevemper Road, straight on at the roundabout to join Edgcumbe Avenue, and under the viaduct; the car park is on the right soon after that. Toilets and a seasonal shop selling ices, sweets, etc., are there. You can get to Trenance Gardens from the centre of Newquay by bus: see current timetables.

1 Starting at the long-stay car park, walk under the Trenance Viaduct (*): there is a short footpath through gardens on the left side of the road. Cross the road at the pedestrian crossing (traffic lights), and now you can walk beside the canalised stream through more gardens, resplendent with well-tended flower beds. (The word "Trenance", a very common place-name in Cornwall, simply means "farmstead in the valley".) A former malthouse on the right was adapted as the Trenance Cottages Museum to contain the collection of assorted curios that had previously been displayed aboard boats laid up in the Gannel: see the note on The Two "Ada"s. Following a burglary towards the end of the 1992 season, the museum was closed and its remaining contents sold at auction. After crossing Trenance Road you reach the boating lake.

THE TRENANCE VIADUCT

The original Trenance (or Tolcarne) Valley viaduct was built in 1849 as part of Treffry's mineral tramway: see the notes on Newquay Harbour (Walk 5) and Treffry's Mineral Railway (Walk 9). The viaduct was locally nicknamed "The Spider", presumably because it looked nearly as fragile as a spider's web, having been built at maximum speed and with minimum expense (in great contrast to the magnificent all-granite viaduct-cum-aqueduct Treffry used to cross the Luxulyan Valley: see Walk 12 in *Around the River Fowey)*. It was, of course, intended for use only by horse-drawn wagons. There is a fine old photograph of it in John Vaughan's *The Newquay Branch and its Branches* (Haynes, 1991); see also *NPP* page 62. Incidentally, the dangers of believing what you read in print are illustrated by the fact that Mr Vaughan gives the length of the viaduct as 147 yards and its height as 58 feet, whereas the figures given by R. J. Woodfin in *The Cornwall Railway* (1960; reprinted by Bradford Barton, 1972) are 210 yards long and 98 feet high! It was rebuilt twice - first in 1874 using masonry piers and wrought-iron girders instead of the original timber, to take the extra weight of the locomotives of the Cornwall Minerals Railway (see page 63 of Hilda Hambly's *North Cornwall Reflections* [Bossiney, 1992] and pages 25 and 33 of Vaughan's book for photographs of it in that form); and finally in 1938-9 as an all-masonry structure with room for a double track in anticipation of hordes of holidaymakers - though as it turned out their arrival was to be delayed for several years by World War 2.

This was created during the early 1930s. Colin Gregory's *Cornwall Since 1900* includes a press photograph of the future King Edward VIII (later the Duke of Windsor) watching men digging the lake out with hand-held forks and shovels. The caption in the *Western Morning News* read: "The Prince of Wales has taken a keen interest in the problems of the unemployed, watching men at work constructing a lake in Trenance gardens. Rather than be idle they are giving their services voluntarily." The same photograph is in *NPP* (page 61), opposite another one, unfortunately not dated, showing the Trenance Valley as seen from the viaduct - an amazingly rural scene. As you approach the far end of the lake, notice the stone building now in use as a garage, on the other side of Trevemper Road, at the corner of Mellanvrane Lane. That road name is a clue to what the old building once was: Mellanvrane means "crow mill", a name that was also given to the chief watermill at Angarrack, near Hayle. The area now occupied by the lake was marsh, flooded at high water, and corn was brought to the mill for grinding by boat. On one occasion an exceptionally high tide meant that the miller and his family had to be rescued through the roof. Continue walking round the end of the lake, past the concrete shelter, to emerge from the gardens near the stables on Trenance Lane and the Rawley Point guest house. The older guide books give that name as "Raleigh Point", and the author of one (Sir Robert Edgcumbe, writing in about 1927) speculates about a possible link with Sir Walter Raleigh, who "at one time owned Crantock." What is fairly certain is that a family called Raleigh owned land here as long ago as the 13th century. Continue to Gannel Road, formerly a quiet little back-road but now part of the busy Gannel Link Road to the western side of Newquay town centre. Cross with care at the traffic island a few yards to the right, and this

Mellanvrane Mill, some time before the building of Trevemper Road in 1929. The track on the right is now Mellanvrane Lane, and the marshy foreground is now the boating lake. Compare the later picture on page 63 of "Newquay's Pictorial Past".

will bring you to the ramp leading down to a footbridge over the Gannel. For a note about the Gannel, see Walk 6.

2 Cross the bridge and bear right. Watch your step: there are occasional small pools and gullies, and many boggy patches, especially where horses from the nearby riding centre have churned up the surface. *(Depending on the weather and the time of the month, the foreshore can be very boggy indeed. Mr Gerry Walters, Vice-Chair of the Newquay Footpaths and Open Spaces Committee, has suggested to me that in this case it would be better to walk along the shore on the opposite [Newquay] side, crossing the Gannel by the lower bridge or the ferry operating there. There is access to the shore near Cairn Cottage on the link road.)* On the Crantock side the best route for walkers seems to be close to the curving main channel of the river, rather than near the low cliffs. (At the point where the river curves left you may notice at foreshore level a small tunnel, about five feet high, in the cliffs; it looks man-made, and could perhaps be the "adit" or drainage-tunnel of a mine. The note about the Gannel in Walk 6 refers to lead- and silver-mining in this area, some of it very ancient; but as far as I know most of the mining was on the other side of the river, and nearer to the sea than this. Perhaps this excavation has something to do with an old mine called North Cargoll, but the workings of that are thought to have been further east, at Trevemper. Even so, I think mining is a more likely explanation than smuggling, despite the fact that alleged smugglers' tunnels seem to have been a feature of almost every Cornish port and inlet.) The tower on the skyline opposite is not a hideous modern church but Newquay Fire Station. Some of the new houses on the slopes on the same side a little further down-river are on the site of the recently-excavated Bronze Age settlement at Trethellan.

3 On reaching Penpol Creek (where the lower footbridge across the Gannel is), continue towards the coast. A few rough stepping stones enable you to cross the Penpol stream more-or-less dryfoot. Close to these you may be able to make out bits of the wrecks of two small ships, both named *Ada* (*). The path now runs up to the cliff-top. This is National Trust property, as announced on the kissing-gate you soon come to. On the opposite side of the Gannel now are hotels and villas set among well-stocked, steeply-sloping gardens; in contrast close at hand are relatively untouched-looking areas of scrub and woodland. Soon you will see where the lower Gannel ferry operates, linking Crantock Beach with the Fern Pit on the Newquay side. Now the path widens to a track and curves inland above the beach car park,

---

THE TWO 'ADA'S

The stories of these two vessels are told in some detail by Martin Langley and Edwina Small in *Lost Ships of the West Country* (Stanford, 1988). "*Ada* (1)" was a two-masted schooner built in 1876. After many years carrying coal and china clay she was moored on the Newquay side of the Gannel in 1928: see the postcard reproduced on page 55. Mr Roger Lacy believes that she was used as the committee boat in several Gannel regattas. She changed ownership several times, was moved to the Crantock side and eventually converted into a house-boat, part of which was open to the public as a curio museum. During the late '40s she suffered severe damage in an accidental fire, and in the mid '50s the remains, which had become potentially dangerous, were intentionally set ablaze, leaving only slight traces above the sands for the sharp-eyed to detect. Her owner bought an ex-RN motor launch in 1948, moored her next to the old ship, renamed her *Ada,* and again converted her into a house-boat-cum-museum. When she eventually became too decrepit to repay more repairs she was put to the torch in her turn. (According to David Szewczuk's *Town Trail* she was destroyed in a

The second *Ada* moored in the Gannel

gale in 1974.) Langley and Small say "The slender remains of this second *Ada* can still be seen a few yards to the south of her predecessor" - though perhaps like me you will have difficulty in finding them.

passing the seasonal café-cum-shop. Continue up Beach Road into Crantock. Some details about this part of the walk are given in sections 1 and 2 of Walk 8, where there is also a note on Crantock.

4 When you reach the old pound and the telephone box, take the minor road called Vosporth Hill, which leads down to Penpol Creek. Where the road turns right at a wayside cross (see Walk 6, end of section 2), you could save a few yards by crossing the concrete-block stile and using the signed "Footpath to Newquay", which soon brings you back to the lane lower down; alternatively, continue on the road and after a hundred yards or so turn left, downhill. Ignore the later "Footpath to Newquay" sign: keep to the lane, which soon brings you to the stepping-stones at the head of the creek.

5 *(On your right as you reach them there is a path running beside the stream, and a wooden stile, beyond which the path climbs gently through a very pretty little valley: see the photograph on the back cover. You may think it's worth a short diversion to enjoy this pleasant spot - but to continue the walk I am suggesting you will need to retrace your steps to the stepping-stones.)*
Cross the stream and climb the small slate stile beside the gate on your right, marked Little Trevithick. The path now consists of a farm track running on the left side of the Penpol stream (though this may hardly be visible in summer) until the track reaches a gateway and leads up to and through Little Trevithick farmyard, leaving that via a metal farm gate. Now the path continues ahead with the hedge to the right. The view to the left is restricted by the nearby hill, though the houses of Newquay are visible; to the right on the skyline is the Trevella Caravan Park, and in the distance can be seen the new "wind farm" at Carland Cross. After more gates you will pass Treringey (said with a hard g) Farm; still continue straight ahead. The view ahead now extends to the "china clay mountains" north of St Austell; just to the right of the windmills, and a little closer, is the church tower at St Newlyn East; the spire further right again is that of Cubert church. On your left (just beyond the brow of the hill, so not visible) are the remains of an Iron Age hill fort or defended settlement known as Treringey Round, well sited to keep watch over the Gannel - just one of five such settlements known to have existed within a mile or so, although it seems to be the only one marked on the Pathfinder map. After the wooden stile, keep on ahead with the hedge on your left; beyond the slate stile the path cuts across to the right-hand side of the field and leaves it at the bottom corner, via a gate.

6 At the T-junction, turn right if you want to look at Trevemper Farm and hamlet, where there are some attractive old houses (there is a brief comment on the former importance of Trevemper in the note about the Gannel in Walk 6); but to continue the walk turn left. Ahead now, beyond the Trenance Viaduct, are the houses of the northern part of Newquay, and you may be able to spot St Columb Minor church tower in the distance. As the track starts to descend you get a bird's eye view of the boating lake and the meandering Gannel river; then as the track becomes a path curving left you see the busy Gannel Link Road, and at last the main Gannel valley approaching the sea.

7 When you get down to river-level, turn right for the footbridge you crossed at the start.

WALK 8
CRANTOCK, HOLYWELL, THE KELSEYS, PORTH JOKE AND WEST PENTIRE

About six miles, or two walks of three miles:
see the instructions at the end.

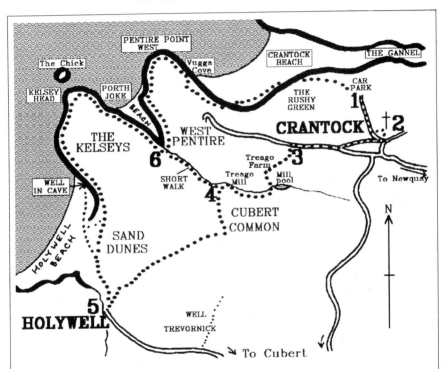

Based on the attractive old village of Crantock, this walk starts by crossing open common land and dunes with wide views, but most of it is along an exceptionally impressive and unspoilt stretch of coastline. I ought to warn you that in a few places the path goes quite close to some sheer drops, and if a strong wind is blowing - particularly an easterly - it might be wiser to choose an inland walk. Very little road walking is involved, there are few steep hills, and you are unlikely to be bothered much by mud. Shops, pubs, cafés and toilets are conveniently placed at Crantock, Holywell and West Pentire (but pub food is not available in Crantock out of season), and you have a choice of three good bathing beaches - but please note that all of them can be dangerous, and it is essential to follow the instructions of the lifeguard services if you intend to enter the water. Take a torch and time your walk to coincide with low water at Holywell if you want to look for the well in the cave there.

CRANTOCK

"At Crantock," I was told by a lady at the Gallery of Old Newquay, "you can't put a spade in the ground without turning up bones." It was important as a port long before Newquay existed. St Carantoc or Caratocus was a Welsh or Irish scholar-bishop who studied under St Patrick. He is said to have come to Cornwall in 460 with a large group of Irish hermits, founded an oratory and eventually died here. Over the succeeding centuries "Lan Garroc" became an important place of pilgrimage and seat of learning. Charles Henderson writes of "the Celtic landowning monastery" that was here before Domesday but "fell a prey to the rapacity of the Norman Earl of Mortain" who seized its lands. A college of priests consisting of a Dean and nine Canons or Prebendaries was founded in about 1236. In 1283 the Collegiate Church was declared the mother church of the whole area now called Newquay and St Columb Minor. "In 1328," writes Henderson, "report reached the bishop's ears that some of the canons of Crantock .... had let their Prebends, lands and houses belonging to the Sanctuary of the church to lay persons who inhabited the houses with their wives, families and servants, even establishing taverns therein, from which strife, contention, wounds and blows proceeded." Various inquiries and punishments followed, but by 1352 things seem to have been as bad as ever: the historian F. E. Halliday even suggests that some of the houses were employed as brothels. A complete reorganisation of the College followed. The Norman church, which had a tower at the centre, was enlarged when it became Collegiate, but by about 1393 it had suffered such neglect that the tower collapsed, bringing down most of the nave with it. About twenty years later, the existing tower was built at the west end. According to the early 19th century historian, Gilbert, an illustrious pupil of the monastic school was John Tregonwell, who earned the favour of Henry VIII "in ridding him," as Halliday puts it, "of two of his superfluous wives." Later he was a leading figure in the suppression of the monasteries during the late 1530s, but the collegiate houses were spared until 1547. During the next three centuries the church fell into ruin again, until at last it was rescued by George Metford Parsons, Vicar from 1894 to 1924. He employed the architect Edmund Sedding and created what John Betjeman describes as "a complete period piece of 1902 and a most sensitive reconstruction, in the imagination of its time, of an old Cornish church." He calls it "one of the most attractive churches in Cornwall"; but admittedly you have to go inside to appreciate this fact, because from the outside the roofline looks clumsy, and the pebbledashed tower could almost be of the same vintage as many of the bungalows nearby. Apparently this finish is the best for standing up to the fierce, salt-laden winds. Outside the main door is a small, circular, carved granite stone, set up like a table-top. Charles Henderson is confident that this "is part of a 16th century mill", and I'm sure he's right, but I prefer Mrs Aldis's more colourful theory that it was a table on which were set out "saints' bones" at a time when such relics were venerated. Two curiosities signposted in the churchyard are the open stone coffin, sometimes said to be that of St Carantoc; and the stocks, with the story of William Tinney's escape from them.

Crantock village well, sometimes called "St Carantoc's Well"

Crantock (*) is signposted from the A3075 Redruth / Truro road soon after it crosses the Gannel at Trevemper bridge. There is no room for parking in the village centre, so follow the signs to the beach, where there is a large car park. Western National bus service No. 87 links Newquay and Crantock, but not on Sundays, and even on weekdays there are very few buses out of season. Please check the current timetable.

1 Return to the car park entrance and walk back up Beach Road, taking special care, since this tends to be very busy in summer. As you approach the church, notice the well beside the entrance to the first house on the left, Penare. This is the one referred to in Miss Husband's *Old Newquay* as the "Sailor's Well". The quaintly carved wooden door is modern; so, too, is the lettering claiming this to be "St Ambrew's Well". St Ambrosius or Ambrusca was probably a follower of St Carantoc. His or her Holy Well was a little further up the hill on the right, in what is now the garden of St Ambros. This we were told by Mrs K. M. Aldis, a lady whose family, the Martyns of Tregonwell or Tregunnel (referred to in Lake's Parochial History), has been associated with Crantock for longer than most, and who remembers it vividly from her childhood. William Hals (1690) wrote of a consecrated arched well of St Ambrosius; slate taken from the stone arch is said to have been used for the doorsteps of the house. When this part of Beach Road was dug up so that water mains could be laid, dozens of skulls, skeletons and coffin-slates were unearthed; apparently the blown sand which once covered this area made it ideal for burying victims of the Black Death. Take the lane on the left, opposite cottages called Pensilva and Belleisle. The cottages on the left are supposed to be on the site of a medieval bakery; Mrs Mogridge, who owns one of them, assured me that her cottage is sometimes filled with the smell of new bread when nobody now living has been doing any baking. Soon you come to Crantock's two pubs, and the church's lych gate is on your left. Do try to make time to visit the church.

2 When you are ready to go on, walk along the road flanked by the two pubs. The more modern one, the Seagull, built where once there was a delightful little orchard, opens only during the summer; the Old Albion is, indeed, old, and pretty too, but when we asked for the menu there in October 1989 we were told, "We don't do food here in the winter." The Cosy Nook Tea Gardens are also seasonal. On the left just past them are some of Crantock's oldest buildings. The first, now a garage or shed, used to be one of the village's two malthouses, and that marks the corner of the block where, Mrs Aldis suggested, the medieval college probably stood. The rather odd circular patch of waste ground surrounded by a high hedge, called the Pound, belongs to the National Trust. Once it was used for impounding stray cattle; Mrs Aldis believes it marks the site of an ancient "Round" or fortified earthwork like Treringey Round, a mile or two to the west. (See Walk 7.) At the corner of Beach Road, near the pretty thatched cottages, is a well covered by a little beehive-like stone roof. Some of the books about Holy Wells identify this as St Carantoc's Well, but for centuries it was merely the main village well, and no-one now can be sure where the saint's baptismal well was. The whitewashed cottage opposite, one of the oldest in Crantock, was originally a thatched farmhouse; inside is a cupboard used by smugglers. The two cottages on the left were formerly stables, and where the gift shop now is was once a round house where a pony went round and round operating a corn-grinding wheel. Go a few yards down Beach Road and then take the first turning left, Gustory Road (called Starry Lane in the days before all the new building). Where this joins the road to West Pentire, continue ahead.

3 Turn left where signposted to Treago Farm. The village on the skyline ahead now is Cubert, whose church spire has for centuries acted as a valuable landmark for sailors. Further right and rather closer is a prominent Bronze Age burial mound or barrow. In *Stories of the North Cornish Coast,* Donald Bray writes of the antiquity of Treago farmhouse, and of its importance to the local smuggling trade; and S. Teague Husband in *Old Newquay* tells how as a girl she explored a tunnel which started at Crantock Beach and ended in the kitchen at Treago. William Hals (1690) wrote that Treago "was heretofore privileged with the jurisdiction of a court leet, and a strong prison for keeping prisoners for debt in durance." Soon after the farm-cum-campsite, the lane brings you to the National Trust sign, Cubert Common (*). Go through the gate, and after crossing the stream follow the main track curving to the right. After a while you will see Treago Mill (*) on your right. Continue along the main track as it bears left.

CUBERT COMMON

Robert Hunt's *Popular Romances of the West of England* (1865) recounts the legend that Cubert Common or the adjoining dunes, or both, was or were once the site of a town with seven churches, called Langona or Langarrow; it is said to have been buried in sand during a storm lasting three days and nights as a punishment for the greed and dissolute behaviour of its people. The tale is probably linked with stories of bells ringing beneath the sand among the dunes south of Holywell, where two churches of St Piran have been buried by the shifting sands at various times, like St Enodoc's church on the Camel estuary north-east of Padstow. There is a similar legend of a buried city at Lelant, near St Ives. (See *A View from Trencrom*, Walk 8.) Cubert Common, a favourite area for horse-riding, is renowned as a good place for cowslips, which flourish better on this lime-rich earth, created by blown sand, than on Cornwall's usual acid soils.

TREAGO MILL

The mill building stands behind the three holiday homes, and the remains of the 20-foot-diameter waterwheel were still in place late in 1992. D.E.Benney's *An Introduction to Cornish Watermills* shows the mill in 1972, already a dilapidated building. A millpond was dug nearby as far back as 1200, and the mill itself is mentioned in 1301. Stories dating back about 300 years tell of smugglers hiding contraband in the mill. The name is pronounced "Tray-go", as in "Trago Mills".

(For the short walk back to Crantock, see the note at the end.)

4 For Holywell, keep on the main track as it bends round to the left, past a small quarry. Ignore the first path off to the right, but when the track curves left towards a group of buildings, keep straight on along a grassy path towards a farm gate. Now take the uphill track furthest to the right (not the small path beside the spring and stream). This leads up to a wall topped by a wire fence, and the path now runs to the left beside the wall. Go through the gate beside a National Trust sign, The Kelseys, and continue with the wall now on your left; beyond it is a golf course. After the kissing gate the path bears slightly left and brings you down into Holywell (*), which has two cafés and two pubs. The Treguth Inn, a little way inland up the road to the left, is much older and more picturesque than the St Piran's Inn by the beach, but both offer a good range of well-prepared food. An old photograph exists showing Treguth farmhouse before its transformation into the Treguth Inn: see page 10 in John N. Rosewarne's *Bygone Cornwall* (Bradford Barton, 1970). "The farmer of Treguth," writes Mr Rosewarne, "was so little bothered with traffic that his cows were able to seek shade and coolness on the beach."

5 Now make for Holywell beach by turning right immediately beyond the St Piran's Inn. After crossing the two wooden bridges, you are faced with a confusing choice of paths over the dunes.

Going left or straight on takes you to the beach, where if the tide is low and still falling you may wish to look for the cave containing one of the two wells which may have given Holywell its name. "This," says P. O. Leggatt in

HOLYWELL

There may have been a Celtic saint called Cubert, or something similar. Catherine Rachel John *(The Saints of Cornwall)* believes the name is a corruption of "Gwbert", who hailed from the Cardigan area. Another theory is that the saint associated with Cubert village and Holywell is Cuthbert of Lindisfarne in Northumberland, which of all places in England is about the furthest away. The story, or legend, is that about a century after his death in 687, the monks of Lindisfarne had to flee because of Viking raids. They sailed for Ireland, taking with them the remains of St Cuthbert, but storms drove them ashore at a place called Porth Reylen or Porraylan ("cove of a little estuary"?), just south of Kelsey Head, where there was already a holy well. St Cuthbert's "reliques accidentally touched the well and to it communicated their qualities." Later the monks were told in a dream to return northwards; they travelled overland to Durham and laid the Saint's remains to rest in the cathedral. No-one knows for sure which of the two "holy wells" nearby gave the seaside settlement its name. The O.S. Pathfinder map marks the one on the beach simply as "Cave", whereas the inland well, north of Trevornick, is labelled "Holy Well (restored)". (The restoration was carried out by Newquay Old Cornwall Society.) This one is on land owned by the Trevornick Holiday Park. As for Holywell itself, the trade in holidays and retirement homes has made something of a shanty-town of it, and the dominant presence of the army, based at Penhale Camp, hardly improves matters. There are compensations, though: the old, or at least "olde worlde", Treguth Inn; the strangely beautiful, ever-shifting sandhills; the splendid beach; the magnificent cliff scenery both north and south; and the fascinating evidence of mining activity around Penhale and Ligger headlands. For details of this last, see *A View from St Agnes Beacon,* Walk 4.

The Healing Wells, "is a famous and probably one of the most beautiful and unique natural healing wells in Cornwall." Before you venture inside, make doubly sure there is no immediate risk of being trapped by the sea. If you have a copy of *A View from St Agnes Beacon,* please accept my apologies for having sent you to the wrong side of the beach. The cave is a rather insignificant-looking one with a low, sloping roof, in a small rocky inlet close to low-water mark on the right (north) side. Some rough steps have been cut into the rock on the left side of the entrance, and these ascend to a small pool surrounded by thick, colourful mineral deposits; more steps lead up to other pools or basins, and finally to a tiny upper chamber. Many scholars say this couldn't have been St Cubert's (or Cuthbert's) well, but for centuries parents have brought their sick or deformed children to be cured, and there are tales of cripples leaving their crutches in the cave. William Hals wrote in about 1690, "The virtues of this water are very great. It is incredible what numbers in summer season frequent this place and waters from counties far distant." Joseph Polsue in his *Lake's Parochial History,* however, describes scientific tests which showed there was "nothing remarkable" in the water. A photograph on page 18 of Joan Rendell's *North Cornwall in the Old Days* (Bossiney, 1983), captioned "A picnic on Holywell Beach", in fact shows people visiting the well; their clothing suggests the 1920s.

THE KELSEYS

Kelsey Head shows signs of ancient habitation, in the forms of the remains of cliff-castle ramparts and barrows (burial mounds), and shaped flints and pieces of early pottery have been found. "The Kelseys" is the name given to the three enclosed fields south of the headland, whose dividing walls seem to be medieval. According to the National Trust leaflet, their design (almost vertical on one side, gently sloping on the other) resembles Dartmoor walling designed to keep deer out, but to let them escape if they did get in. The meaning of "Kelsey" is unknown.

Going right from the bridges takes you towards the cliffs; please use the "sand ladders" where they have been laid, and avoid trampling the marram grass which is an essential defence against wind erosion. Eventually, I hope, you will reach a kissing gate near the cliff edge on the west side of The Kelseys (*). From here the coastal footpath is clear. It's worth taking the side paths to the cliff edges, as long as you have a good head for heights: the jet-black rocks make a fine contrast with the white foam, and the flowers - thrift, cowslips, primroses, according to season - can be breathtaking. Rabbits abound up here, hawks hover, skylarks soar - and, of course, the seabirds throng in their thousands. Soon there is a good view ahead of Porth ("Polly") Joke (*) and the coast beyond. Keep to the cliff path as it curves south-east beside Porth Joke; or, if the tide is low enough, you could cut across the beach, but you may have to negotiate various pools and streams, and the way up to the coast path on the far side involves quite a steep and awkward scramble up rocks and a sandy path.

PORTH JOKE

For many people, the loveliest beach near Newquay, saved from development by its inaccessibility to road vehicles, and now also by the National Trust. Its name is of particular interest. Just as *porth* could mean "cove", so too could *pol;* hence, presumably, the alternative name, "Polly Joke". Many explanations of "joke" have been offered, including "creek" (from *gwic)*, "chough" (the crow-like bird once so common in Cornwall as to become an emblem of the County, but now extinct here), and "plants" (from *les;* not much like the word "joke", I agree, but this is the explanation given by the leading authority on Cornish place-names, Oliver Padel).

6 To continue round the coast, go through the kissing gate beyond the footbridge (assuming, of course, that you kept to the cliff path rather than crossing the beach) and turn left on to the narrower path which follows the cliff edge. As you approach Pentire Point West, for the best views use the lower, left-hand path which keeps closer to the edge. This will enable you to see the collapsed cave, a gaping hole beside the path just after it has rounded the headland: the cave's roof has apparently been blown off by the pressure of air built up by storm-driven seas rushing into the cave. Further round, this lower path brings you down to the rocks above Vugga Cove (*), and you can walk down to water-level or the tiny beach there via one of the two rough slipways. From there the path curves up very steeply to rejoin the main one;

VUGGA COVE

The name of this inlet means "cave" (from the same Cornish original as the word "fogou", used by archaeologists to refer to early cave-like structures). Perhaps it was once a cave, but the main points of interest now are the two slipways hacked out of the rocks, and the ruined storage shed at the top of one of them; there are also some old mooring rings set in the rocks. It is difficult now to envisage Vugga Cove as a practicable harbour; Brian Le Messurier's National Trust leaflet mentions two possible explanations (the launching of pilot gigs and the shipping of slate quarried nearby), but no solid information seems to have come to light. The tithe map of 1839 names the field beside the building as Cellar Field, so this may have been the site of a fish cellar.

until/unless some steps are cut, you might find it better to return the way you came to get back to the higher path. Soon you will see, up on the right, the hamlet - now mainly a holiday village - of West Pentire, and one of the most prominent buildings is the Bowgie Inn (recognisable by its pink-washed walls in 1989, but of course that may change); a path leads to it from the cliffs, via the pub's car park. A good food menu is available, and on sunny days you can enjoy sea views from the picnic tables outside. The West Pentire Café is also nearby. Continuing along the coastal footpath, you could follow the acorn signs as the path runs up and down around several inlets above Crantock Beach, but if the tide is low enough I would recommend you to get down to the beach at the first opportunity (there's an easy way down at the

first main inlet). The sand is firm, and you have a good view of the black cliffs, plus a chance to explore some caves. Continue along below the sandhills (called "The Rushy Green"). Probably the quickest way back to the car park is to climb up behind the white huts belonging to the Crantock Surf Life Saving Club and walk along the sand-ladder. When that ends, continue ahead along the main path, heading towards the large camp-site on the skyline, and without too much trouble you should find the steps leading down to the car park.

SHORTER ROUTES

OMITTING HOLYWELL AND THE KELSEYS

At point 4, instead of turning left go straight on over the stile, through the car park, through the gate by the National Trust sign, The Kelseys, and down the attractive and surprisingly wide valley, where willows and water-plants flourish beside the stream. After about half a mile you reach Porth Joke; now pick up the directions from point 6.

OMITTING CRANTOCK AND WEST PENTIRE

Start at Holywell; there are at least two car parks near the beach, one belonging to the National Trust. Follow section 5 of the directions; at Porth Joke continue up the inland path with the stream on your left. After about half a mile, pass through the small car park. Finally follow section 4 of the directions - except, of course, that from this angle the track at the start is on your right.

Polly Joke

WALK 9
TRERICE, GWILLS AND TREWERRY MILL

About three miles

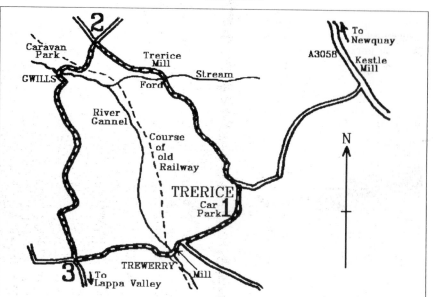

This short, fairly easy walk is good for wet weather conditions, because the whole route is on roads - narrow back-roads in an area so peaceful and rural that it is very hard to believe that the centre of Newquay is only two or three miles away. I called the walk <u>fairly</u> easy because the area is quite hilly. The walk is based on Trerice Manor, one of the finest Tudor houses in Cornwall, now in the care of the National Trust, and since you can complete the walk in well under two hours, it can conveniently be combined with a visit to the house and garden. There is ample parking there, and refreshments are available in the Barn. The walk route twice crosses the course of a disused railway with an interesting history, three times crosses the River Gannel or its tributary streams, and passes two picturesque mills. The second of those, Trewerry, has a Tea Garden and Tea Room, and is a particularly attractive spot; refreshments are served between 10.30 and 5.30 every day between Spring Bank Holiday and the end of September, and also during Easter week. Between then and Spring Bank Holiday you can get refreshments only on Fridays, Saturdays and Sundays.

TRERICE MANOR

Unlike most "stately homes", Trerice manages to feel homely as well as being impressive and beautiful. Its sheltered site had the benefit of a strong and reliable spring. The manor house and estate of 500 acres became the property of the Arundell family (see the note on St Mawgan, Walk 2) in the 14th century, and the fourth Sir John Arundell completed his re-building of the old house in 1573. His son achieved fame as

Governor of Pendennis Castle, Falmouth, withstanding a five-month siege by Fairfax's army in 1646 before surrendering with honour; eventually Charles II recognised this loyal service by creating the title of Baron Arundell of Trerice. When the male line of the Arundell family ceased in the 18th century, Trerice passed to the Wentworths and later to the Aclands, who finally sold it in 1915. Most of the estate was divided into small farms, but in 1953 the house with 20 acres was bought by the National Trust, who refurnished it and carried out restoration work. Notice the elaborate Dutch-style gables, which are unique in Elizabethan architecture; the only explanation for them that I have heard is that Sir John may have seen and admired similar ones when on military service in Holland. The Great Hall is dominated by its huge mullioned window, which has 576 panes of glass, many of them the original ones; notice too the massive fireplace and mantel, the fine oak table dating from the 19th century, and the Musicians' Gallery above, where the performers can be heard but not seen. (A small choir my wife and I belong to, Trerice Minstrels, once sang madrigals there to entertain guests below, but they carried on chatting, and afterwards one of them asked what that nice tape was!) The plaster ceiling is very fine, but has been much restored; the true "glory of the house", as the guide-book puts it, is the plaster barrel ceiling of the Drawing-Room upstairs, which is still in its original state. The outbuildings reflect Trerice's history as a working farm: the Great Barn, now a restaurant, once had stables at one end and a grinding-mill plus cider press at the other, with an area for threshing corn in between. Another outbuilding now houses a surprising collection of old lawn-mowers. The colourful gardens complete the pleasure of a visit to Trerice.

To drive to Trerice (*) from Newquay, take the A3059 and A392 to Quintrell Downs, and continue straight ahead along the A3058 for about one more mile to Kestle Mill. Trerice is signposted on the right from there, along narrow roads where careful driving is called for. Continue past the main entrance of the house to the National Trust car park, on the right. There are no bus services to Trerice.

1 From the entrance to the car park - or from the main gateway, if you decide to visit the house first - turn left, then left again, following the sign: Legonna, Lane and Newquay. Soon you pass the rear entrance to the house, and later two small farms, once part of the Trerice estate. Gradually the road descends to a ford and footbridge, and just beyond is Trerice Mill. The present owners, Mr and Mrs Schofield, believe that it dates from the 17th century and was probably a saw-mill. A leat fed a reservoir, parts of which still remain, behind the house. The granite wall on the right of the house is inscribed "Trerice" plus a date which looks like 1794. Continue up the road, past Legonna Farm.

2 At the crossroads turn left, signposted to Gwills. The road descends to two bridges; the first crosses the disused railway (*) and the second the River Gannel (see the note in Walk 6). Nearby is the attractively secluded Gwills caravan park. (The name is probably from Cornish *guel,* an open field.) Now there is quite a long uphill stretch with good views developing: as you approach the top, look back to see Newquay, and left to see Trerice, on the left-hand edge of the wood in the middle distance. A little further south (right) is the Lappa Valley, where Treffry's mineral line has been transformed

---

TREFFRY'S MINERAL RAILWAY

For the main note about Joseph Thomas Treffry, see Walk 5. February 1849 saw the opening of his tramway (railway for use by horse-drawn wagons) connecting Newquay harbour with the great lead mine at East Wheal Rose (see Walk 1 in *A View from St Agnes Beacon),* and the Trerice walk twice crosses the course of this. Later a line linking Newquay to St Dennis, at the heart of china-clay country, was opened. (June 1849 is the date given by John Keast, John Vaughan and other writers, but Mr Roger Lacy, who has studied contemporary newspaper articles and letters, has concluded that the link with St Dennis was not made till 1857, seven years after Treffry's death.) In 1873 these "tramways" were bought up by the Cornwall Minerals Railway, converted for use by steam locomotives, and the East Wheal Rose line was extended to Treamble to serve the iron mines: see Walk 4 in the same book. But there was less demand for the railway's services than had been expected, and before long the line was taken over by the Great Western in order to complete their route from Chacewater via St Agnes and Perranporth to Newquay. This was eventually axed by Beeching in the 1960s, and the chance to convert it into an attractive footpath was missed. Lewis Reade's *Branch Line Memories,* Volume 1: Great Western (1983), and *The Branch Lines of Cornwall* (1984 - both published by Atlantic) contain features on the Chacewater to Newquay line; so too does *The Newquay Branch and its Branches* by John Vaughan (Haynes, 1991).

into a miniature railway. Continue past the entrance to Polgreen ("gravel pit") Farm and round a double bend at Polgreen Vean (Little Polgreen).

3 At the crossroads (Trevoll or Trevoal) turn left, signposted to Trerice and Kestle Mill, a pretty road leading down to Trewerry, where for a second time you cross both the Gannel and the former railway. The first house on the right is called "Trewerry Halt", and indeed part of the old platform and two level-crossing gates are still there; on the left, half-hidden now among flowers, is the pretty bridge that carried the line. The road bridge, too, is attractive, though spoilt somewhat by the prominent railings. Beyond that is Trewerry Mill (*). To complete the walk, continue along the road for about another half mile, ignoring the right turning soon after the Mill.

TREWERRY MILL

The mill dates back at least to the early 17th century - note the fine doorway dated 1639 - but the house was largely rebuilt in 1820. "Two pairs of mills" were offered on lease in 1808, together with a house, barn, stable and five acres of land, for a rent of £39.50 per annum. The cast-iron overshot waterwheel, 16 feet in diameter, equipped with deep wooden buckets, is unusually well preserved. The house has been in use as a Tearoom since about 1900, and has long been a favourite outing from Newquay. Inside are several interesting old photographs of the mill and of Trewerry and Trerice Halt, the tiny railway station which once stood on the opposite bank of the Gannel.

WALK 10
COLAN CHURCH, FIR HILL
TREGOOSE AND LADY NANCE,
WITH A POSSIBLE EXTENSION TO
PORTH RESERVOIR AND MELANCOOSE

*A choice of routes ranging from about three miles to about six,
plus an extra mile or more beside the reservoir if you wish.*

*This is a gentle and pretty walk, mostly along quiet country roads and paths
through woodland and fields. The starting point is an attractive little
ancient church "in the middle of nowhere"; next comes a track through
beautiful woodland with glimpses of the man-made lake below, passing the
remains of an old manor
house. Next, a steepish
cross-field climb gives a
superb view of the reservoir,
and then a quiet country
road leads down past old
farm buildings to a beautifully
restored old watermill in an
idyllic setting beside a ford.
After another farm, you
could return direct to the
church or add nearly a mile
to the walk by visiting a holy
well and returning to the
church across fields. Finally
you could walk (or, if you
prefer, drive) about a mile to
the public entrance of Porth
Reservoir. Here you can
picnic, get a day-licence for
angling, walk along the*

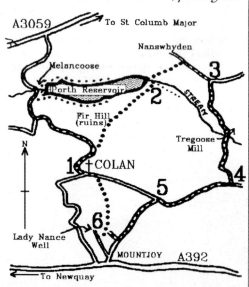

*water's edge - or just admire the view and continue a little further along the
road to another nicely restored old mill. From there, if you walked, you
have to retrace your steps to the church. A few patches on the woodland
paths and tracks are likely to be very muddy, and during wet spells you
would be glad of wellingtons just past the bridge below Nanswhyden; apart
from this, the going is easy. You may have to climb a gate and a fence if you
include Lady Nance Well on the walk. There is no shop along the route.*

Colan Church (grid reference: 868613) is about three miles east of Newquay
and half a mile south of Porth Reservoir; it is mid-way between the A3059
and A392 roads, and is signposted from both. A little roadside parking is
available beside the churchyard. No bus runs to Colan, but Western National
service 91 uses the A392, and the stop at Mountjoy is near Lady Nance Well:
you could then do the complete round walk, starting part-way through point 5
and turning left at St Joseph.

COLAN CHURCH

This is the only English church dedicated to St Colan (or Collen), but there is another in Wales and a third in Brittany: the saint's name is disguised in the place names, Llangollen and Llollen. Legends about St Colan exist, but no solid information, and one theory is that the name Colan actually refers to a pre-Christian fire-god. The church was built about 1250; there were many later changes and additions, including major restoration in 1884. The two 16th-century brasses are worth a close look. The small one on the north wall shows Francis Bluet or Blewett, his wife, and an amazing crowd of children (as Arthur Mee's Cornwall volume in *The King's England* put it: "a seemingly numberless host of 22 children, an odd boy in breeches and all the rest in cloaks, with nine girls in long dresses with dashed sleeves"). The Cosowarth family, including a mere eight children, are commemorated on the south wall; the special point of interest here is a bullet-hole in the brass. The theory that one of Cromwell's supporters took a shot at it is, unfortunately, more probable than the story that a jilted lover fired at his former sweetheart as she stood at the altar to be married to his rival. Outside the church, just to the right of the entrance porch, stands a small 10th-century Cornish cross, very worn and damaged. The story of its discovery and preservation is told on a framed notice at the west end of the church. Many visitors to Colan Church must be puzzled at its very existence, so far from any centre of population, but there were once more cottages nearby, plus several hamlets and important farming families; and since 1974 the congregation has been increased by the addition of Quintrell Downs to the parish.

1 Walk along the road with the church (*) on your right. After a few hundred yards there is a sharp left turn; here, continue straight ahead along a wide track overarched by tall pines - once the entrance drive to a mansion, as will soon be explained. Before long you enter the woods. Ignore the track going left. Soon after this, as the track starts going more noticeably downhill, you will see a ruined building on the left, and a little later several more ruins, at least one of which is quite large. These were once Fir Hill Manor (*); whether the ruined house on the right was also part of the Manor I have not discovered. Keep to the main track, from which - at least during winter when there is little foliage - you get good views of Porth Reservoir with St Columb Minor church on the hill above the dam at the far end.

2 *Just before the bridge, you could make an attractive short diversion to the right - a lovely path (possibly muddy in a few places) among tall trees. Ignore all the side paths to the left. Just beyond the point where the path comes close to the stream you will see evidence of old mining in the form of filled-in shafts in the bank on the right. According to Mr H. Baker, who owns Nanswhyden (*) farm, steam sometimes rises from these shafts, and it's a sure*

NANSWHYDEN AND FIR HILL

For many years, the main landowners in this district were the Hoblyn family. About 1740, Robert Hoblyn, MP for Bristol, built a fine new house at Nanswhyden (pronounced "Nan-Sweden" and meaning "wooded valley"), which despite its name is up on the ridge, where Nanswhyden farmhouse now is. It was equipped with a fine library, and also housed a notable collection of mineral specimens. In December 1802 (1803 according to Polsue's *Lake's Parochial History)* the house was burnt down, and the Hoblyns moved to Fir Hill Manor (#) on the other side of the valley, turning it into what Polsue calls a "pleasant villa residence". According to the leaflet in the church, firs were planted there about 1900 (though the name Fir Hill is much older than that), and it then "became a show place". Eventually, after World War I, the direct male line died out and the house was deserted; Mr Baker of Nanswhyden told me that its last occupants were a girls' school, evacuated to it during World War II. After that it was neglected and vandalised, and now it is what estate agents describe as an ideal opportunity for the handyman. If your name is Hoblyn, this could be your big chance, because the family fortune is awaiting the rightful heir. In 1948 a "loud-talking American with a big Stetson hat" claimed the 1700-acre estate. By name Francis Figg-Hoblyn, he was the eldest son of one of the Squire's daughters who as a teenager had been "packed off" to Canada in 1883 after having an affair with a coachman. Mr Figg-Hoblyn failed to establish his claim, however, and during the 1970s his widow met with similar difficulties. An article in a local paper ("The Courier") in 1978 told the tale of the "Mystery of the Cornish Estate without an Owner", reporting that another potential claimant was Cyril Hoblyn, a sub-postmaster from Blackwater, then aged 83, but he had decided against pursuing his claim because "it would be more of a worry than it is worth."

(#) Whether Fir Hill was truly a manor I am not sure, but it is often referred to as such.

---

sign of rain on the way. He believes that the miners were extracting ochre, and this is confirmed by records of "some tons" of ochre produced by Fir Hill Mine in 1886. The Mining Journal of 1857 reported that the ochre and umber from this area were "admirably suited to paper stainers' purposes". In the 1840s a mine called Wheal Aaron operated here and recovered various minerals including manganese, iron, lead and copper. Mr Baker also thinks an attempt was made to dig a canal in this valley to link it with Porth, and this could have been part of the Mawgan Porth - St Columb Major - Porth canal planned by Edyvean: see Walks 1 and 3. Near the old shafts, the path reaches the stream and stops; return to the main track by the same route.

Beside the bridge, unless recent rains have swollen the stream there is a tiny "beach", ideal for a picnic if the weather's right. To the left is a nature reserve: see the later note about the reservoir. Cross the bridge, negotiate the boggy patch beyond, go diagonally uphill to the right towards the nearest trees on the hilltop, and turn right on the farm drive at the top. Look back for a beautiful view of Porth Reservoir.

3 After the farm gate, turn right, following the sign to Tregoose. This pretty road slopes gently and then more steeply into the wooded valley, passing the attractively restored Tregoose farmhouse before reaching the delightful buildings of Tregoose Old Mill (*) beside the ford. Cross the bridge and walk up past the entrance to Tregoose House.

TREGOOSE MILL

The earliest record of this mill dates from 1562. It was still operative until World War II, when the wheel was taken away for scrap iron. The position of the axle is obvious on the end wall on the right as you face the house, and the owner told me there is still evidence of the mill race on the bank above. Some of the original gearing is displayed beside the front door. The pretty cottage a little higher up the road was probably the miller's house, built about 1800. "Tregoose" means "farm in the wood".

---

4 At the top of the hill, turn right, following the sign to Colan. This brings you to Bosoughan, a busy farm which makes no attempt to be picturesque (like its name, which probably means "pig house") but has an interesting array of buildings in all styles and materials, including a shed with exposed cob walls.

5 At the left turning, signposted Newquay, either go straight on for Colan church, or turn left to visit the old well. This road provides a panoramic view to the coast, with Newquay and the tall tower of St Columb Minor prominent. When you get to the hamlet of Mountjoy (said as "Munjy" by some but by no means all of the locals, and meaning "stone house"), turn right at St Joseph, along a lane with several houses. At the end go left through the gateway and follow the track through the field down to a small wooden gate at the left-hand corner; beyond that you cross a tiny stream and walk along a path made of concrete blocks. At the lane turn right, and after a few yards more blocks lead down on the right to Lady Nance Well (*).

6 Return by the same path at first, but as soon as you reach the field go left by the hedge and through or over the metal farm gate. The path ahead is

LADY NANCE WELL

As the lady and gentleman who helped me find it said, "It's nothing special" to look at now, but once the water was famous as a cure for eye ailments, and according to local tradition you could find out whether or not you would survive the next twelve months by throwing a palm cross in on Palm Sunday. If it floated you were safe - but only if you gave an offering to the vicar. "Lady" must refer to the Virgin Mary; "Nance" has been linked to Nantes in France, but could derive from the Cornish word for a valley, which appears as "Nance" in many other place-names. The little well-house was built in 1910 according to P. O. Leggat in *The Healing Wells*, but in fact it is shown on a card posted in March 1908, and does not look new even then. The card, which is in Mr Roger Lacy's collection, is too faded now to reproduce successfully, so I have based a sketch on it.

clear, running up to an old rusty gate in front of which a wooden fence has been built, and this you will have to climb over unless the barbed-wire has been removed from the gap nearby. Now keep beside the hedge on the left and continue ahead along a cart-track. Turn left at the road, and you are soon back at the church.

A worthwhile extra would be to extend the walk to Porth Reservoir, and then a short way beyond that to another delightful old watermill at Melancoose. The route to them is entirely on roads, and since a public footpath shown on all the maps (running from Trebarber Farm via Treisaac to Nanswhyden) appears to be unusable now, you would have to walk back to Colan the same way, so you might prefer to drive to the reservoir. To get there, set off in the same direction as for the main walk, but continue along the road instead of taking the track to Fir Hill, and take the first turning right.   There is a

PORTH RESERVOIR

The reservoir was opened in 1960, mainly to serve the needs of Newquay. There is no public footpath round the eastern end, because this is kept as a nature reserve to protect bird-life, and there are hides for bird-watchers. During the winter the water-level is kept low for the benefit of wading birds. Licences for fishing can be bought at a shed near the entrance. If you walk round by the dam, notice the water gushing through the feeder pipe. The ranger says it is quite common to see sea-trout (known as "peal" or "peel") on their way upstream to breed, leaping up to the pipe and swimming through it, then resting in the pools above before continuing up through the next pipe into the reservoir.

footpath on each side of the reservoir (you can get to the one on the northern bank by walking to the left of the dam and up steps on the far side), but you cannot do a complete circuit of the lake, as explained in the note. From the main entrance to the reservoir continue down into the valley for Melancoose Mill, with its duckpond, millstones and recently restored or replaced waterwheel. When working, the mill employed a 12-foot overshot wheel. Melancoose, whose name means "mill in the woods", was mentioned in a document as early as 1334.

Melancoose Mill in 1989, before the waterwheel was restored

POSTSCRIPT TO WALK 10

If you can find a copy of James Turner's *The Stone Peninsula* (William Kimber, 1975) I think you will enjoy reading his atmospheric description of Colan, "a hamlet never torn out of its medieval quiet." Mr Turner tells the story of Fir Hill, portraying the ruins as a suitable set for a horror movie; and he calls Lady Nance "one of those secret 'sacred' places which were lit, for people of former ages, with a peculiar light and veneration."

FURTHER READING

Donald Bray	Stories of the North Cornish Coast (Truran 1983)
T. O. Darke	St Eval - Portrait of a Parish (Lodeneck 1991)
Michael Haigh and David Woolgrove	Newquay: The Story of a Cornish Town / Explore Newquay (G. J. Publications, mid-1970s; both now out of print, but well worth seeking out)
S. Teague Husband	Old Newquay (1923; facsimile edition published in 1985 by Dyllansow Truran)
A. K. Hamilton Jenkin	Mines and Miners of Cornwall Volumes 7 and 9 (published during the 1960s and now out of print but obtainable through libraries)
John Keast	The King of Mid-Cornwall: The Life of Joseph Thomas Treffry (1782-1850) (Truran 1982)
Charles Lee	Vale of Lanherne (written about 1903, published in 1984 by Dyllansow Truran)
Brian Le Messurier	Bedruthan and Park Head / Crantock to Holywell Bay (National Trust "Coast of Cornwall" Leaflets)
Newquay Old Cornwall Society	Newquay's Pictorial Past (undated)
Oliver Padel	Cornish Place-Name Elements (English Place-Name Society 1985) and A Popular Dictionary of Cornish Place-Names (Alison Hodge 1988)
Ivan Rabey	The Book of St Columb and St Mawgan (Barracuda Books 1979) (and several other books on topics related to St Columb Major and district, such as hurling, the Vale of Lanherne and R.A.F. St Eval)
Lewis Reade	The Branch Lines of Cornwall (Atlantic 1984)
David Szewczuk	Newquay Town Trail Walkabout (Cornwall Heritage Project 1989)
Nigel Tangye	The Story of Glendorgal (Bradford Barton 1969)
John Vaughan	The Newquay Branch & its Branches (Haynes 1991)
Craig Weatherhill	Cornovia: Ancient Sites of Cornwall & Scilly (Alison Hodge 1985)